Phillip Harris Bryant
Jan 1962
Oxford, Mississippi

CHARLES P. CURTIS

A COMMONPLACE
BOOK

SIMON AND SCHUSTER

1957

LIBRARY OF CONGRESS CATALOG CARD NUMBER:
57-10972
MANUFACTURED IN THE UNITED STATES OF AMERICA
BY KINGSPORT PRESS, INC., KINGSPORT, TENN.

TO MY MOTHER

A COMMONPLACE
BOOK

❋ 1 ❋

"I shall light a candle of understanding in thine heart, which shall not be put out, till the things be performed which thou shalt begin to write."

I LIKE "a *candle* of understanding." Not a flash, nor a searchlight, nor a floodlight. A small flame burning in a great room, flickering and swaying in the drafts, darkening the far corners, casting long shadows behind high-backed chairs, the deeper behind what it most illuminates. A warm light, lending grace and beauty to what it is making visible, and giving a presence to what it leaves obscure.

What has our language done to the meaning of this word *understanding?* Why have we confined its meaning to the completion of a process, and left ourselves with no word for the process itself? As a matter of grammar as well as fact, we are understanding something when we are on our way toward comprehending it. This is what we do, and the word is a present participle.

We have done the same thing with the word *believing.* We have made it mean the same thing as belief, which by rights is a successful believing. Take

1

living. We recognize it as a process, and we make this doubly clear by recognizing that its completion is something quite different—not life, but death. Understanding, likewise, is a process we should be as sorry to complete as we are sure we shan't.

❋ 2 ❋

"It is not in Montaigne, but in me," Pascal said, "that I find all that I see there."

WE ADMIRE and we praise a writer for expressing his thoughts clearly and communicating them to us. But a good reader expects more of a good writer than a clear expression of his thoughts. There is more to language and to literature than that.

Good writers know how much more there is. What Virginia Woolf said about the highest poetry is only less true about lesser poetry, and it is likewise as true of prose as it is of poetry. The only difference between poetry and prose, anyhow, is the tone of your voice when you read them aloud. No, they differ in the scope of their ambitions. Poetry undertakes to express more than it thinks it can. Prose tells you it is expressing less than it knows it can. As you see, I'm no poet.

What Virginia Woolf said was this: "There is an ambiguity which is the work of the highest poetry; we cannot know exactly what it means. . . . The meaning is just on the far side of language; . . . the meaning that Shakespeare succeeds in snaring."

Let the good writer snare it if he can. If he can, so much the better. If he can't, a good reader wants to try and snare something for himself. For we readers are not going to be satisfied with what a writer is able to communicate to us, with only what we must share with him. This would reduce the meaning of what we read to what we have in common with the author, which would come to no more than the lesser of us has to offer. No reader would be willing to take the next step and reduce the meaning of the words he reads to their dictionary definitions. For this would reduce their meaning to the least common denominator of other readers.

The good reader will want to exploit the great fact that understanding outruns expression. Parents know how true this is. A child is more intelligent than it seems to be, if we judge it only by what it says. Likewise we are better poets for ourselves than any but the great poets are for us, in our behalf and in our stead.

Nor does it take a great poet to exploit the genius of the language. For, as I say, there is more to language than expression or communication. Good writing is an instigation, an impregnation. It is invigoration. It is a source of power.

I speak for the reader, and I give him a quotation

which will at the same time state and illustrate my point. "Books, we are told, propose to *instruct* or to *amuse*. Indeed!" And De Quincey went on: "The true antithesis to knowledge, in this case, is not *pleasure*, but *power*. All that is literature seeks to communicate power; all that is not literature, to communicate knowledge."

Literature is a transmission of power. Textbooks and treatises, dictionaries and encyclopedias, manuals and books of instruction—they are communications; but literature is a power line, and the motor, mark you, is the reader.

My metaphor falls short. You read something, and your attention is attracted by a phrase or a sentence or by some passage or other. Or the passage lights up in your memory later. In either case, the reason why may not at once, may not ever, be clearly apparent. If your mind is open, either in perplexity or in some bewilderment or out of sheer curiosity, you will apply yourself to the passage, not trying to force a meaning out of it, nor yet quite letting go of it. What you want is not so much its meaning as its significance to you; and the more of your relevant self you can apply to it, the greater this significance will be.

Coleridge said, "The poet, described in *ideal* perfection, brings the whole soul of man into activity, with the subordination of its faculties to each other, according to their relative worth and dignity. He diffuses a tone and spirit of unity, that blends and (as it were) *fuses*, each into each, by that synthetic

4

and magical power, to which we have exclusively appropriated the name of imagination."

In his Note-books, Coleridge said, "But of Poetry commonly so called we might justly call it—A mode of composition that calls into action and gratifies the largest number of the human Faculties in Harmony with each other, and in just proportions."

I wish the literary pundits—here Coleridge as well as Woolf—would admit that there is more to literature than poetry. We readers are not so snobbish. We know we are exploring ourselves. We are pushing the articulate frontiers of our understanding further into the wilderness of our thought. We are trying to become more aware of ourselves. And there is no end to it. The further our understanding advances, newer horizons lift into view more mountain ranges. The more we understand, the more we perceive of what we do not understand. And on the way we readers are snaring our own meanings. Is there any better way for an explorer to live off the country?

❁ 3 ❁

"In a sense, one can never read the book that the author originally wrote, and one can never read the same book twice."

THIS IS the last sentence of Edmund Wilson's preface to his *The Triple Thinkers*.

Books are like rivers. "You cannot bathe in the same river twice, for new waters are ever flowing in upon you," Heraclitus said.

Or are we readers the rivers? And books the countryside through which we flow?

❁ 4 ❁

The Duke says, in Measure for Measure, "Love talks with better knowledge, and knowledge with dearer love."

IT IS HARD to speak fairer or more precisely.

I think it was Goethe who said you cannot learn to understand anything unless you love it.

Thoreau says, "The only way to speak the truth is to speak lovingly." I do not need to remind you that God lit Esdras' candle of understanding in his heart.

I suppose there must be some things so cold that you can best understand them by approaching them coldly, objects that you do well to examine objectively. The multiplication table, perhaps. But then you are only trying to learn it, not to understand it. A learned treatise, or a guidebook, or a timetable. No, not a dictionary, for you want to make the word you are looking up something more than an acquaintance, even when you want to know only how it is best spelled. A word must become a friend or you will not understand it. Perhaps you do well to be cool and detached when you are seeking information, but I remind you of the wife who complained, "When I ask John if he loves me, he thinks I am asking for information."

Distance may or may not lend enchantment to a view, but it does give you a perspective, a view of the whole. A prejudice serves the same purpose for an idea. It is what you think about the whole of it, for or against, one way or the other, before you go up closer to examine it and take it to pieces. It is your attitude toward it to begin with. If you have any attitude or any thoughts about it, you are prejudiced. And why not? There are only two ways to be quite unprejudiced and impartial. One is to be completely ignorant. The other is to be completely indifferent. Bias and prejudice are attitudes to be kept in hand, not attitudes to be avoided.

I am not confounding understanding with belief. I am not saying that you must believe something in order to understand it. Believing is a very superficial business compared to loving. You can believe something by merely mentally assenting to it or accepting it. What I am saying is that you cannot understand anything without some degree of passion, and I am not at all sure that hate—not fear, but a good sound hatred—may not serve the purpose.

❀ 5 ❀

"The perfect horror story must be about something that cannot happen, must not happen, and does happen."

THIS, ACCORDING to my wife, is Edith Wharton. Since my wife's quotations are usually better than their source, I have not tried to check this one.

Aristotle said that an author should "prefer probable impossibilities to improbable possibilities." Or, in Toynbee's translation, "Prefer what is impossible but plausible, to what is possible but incredible."

❋ 6 ❋

"As soon as the play, which was Hamlet, Prince of Denmark, began, Partridge was all attention, nor did he break silence till the entrance of the ghost; upon which he asked Jones, 'What man that was in the strange dress; something,' said he, 'like what I have seen in a picture. Sure it is not armour, is it?'

"Jones answered, 'That is the ghost.'

"To which Partridge replied, with a smile, 'Persuade me to that, sir, if you can. Though I can't say I ever actually saw a ghost in my life, yet I am certain I should know one, if I saw him, better than that comes to. No, no, sir, ghosts don't appear in such dresses as that, neither.'

"In this mistake which caused much laughter in the neighborhood of Partridge, he was suffered to continue, till the scene between the ghost and Hamlet, when Partridge gave that credit to Mr. Garrick which he had denied to Jones, and fell into so violent a trembling, that his knees knocked against each other.

"Jones asked him what was the matter, and whether he was afraid of the warrior upon the stage? 'O la! sir,' said he, 'I perceive now it is what you told me. I am not afraid of anything; for I know it

9

is but a play. And if it was really a ghost, it could do one no harm at such a distance, and in so much company; and yet if I was frightened, I am not the only person.'

" 'Why, who,' cries Jones, 'dost thou take to be such a coward here besides thyself?'

" 'Nay, you may call me coward if you will; but if that little man there upon the stage is not frightened, I never saw any man frightened in my life. Ay, ay; go along with you! Ay, to be sure! Who's fool then? Will you? Lud have mercy upon such fool-hardiness! Whatever happens, it is good enough for you. Follow you? I'd follow the devil as soon. Nay, perhaps it is the devil; for they say he can put on what likeness he pleases. Oh! here he is again. —No farther! No, you have gone far enough already; farther than I'd have gone for all the king's dominions.'

"Jones offered to speak, but Partridge cried, 'Hush, hush! dear sir, don't you hear him?' And during the whole speech of the ghost, he sat with his eyes fixed partly on the ghost and partly on Hamlet, and with his mouth open; the same passions which succeeded each other in Hamlet succeeding likewise in him.

"When the scene was over Jones said, 'Why, Partridge, you exceed my expectations. You enjoy the play more than I conceived possible.'

" 'Nay, sir,' answered Partridge, 'if you are not afraid of the devil, I can't help it; but, to be sure, it is natural to be surprised at such things, though

10

I know there is nothing in them: not that it was the ghost that surprised me, neither; for I should have known that to have been only a man in a strange dress; but when I saw the little man so frightened himself, it was that which took hold of me.'

" 'And dost thou imagine, then, Partridge,' cries Jones, 'that he was really frightened?'

" 'Nay, sir,' said Partridge, 'did not you yourself observe afterwards, when he found it was his own father's spirit, and how he was murdered in the garden, how his fear forsook him by degrees; and he was struck dumb with sorrow, as it were, just as I should have been, had it been my own case? But hush! O la! what noise is that? There he is again.— Well, to be certain, though I know there is nothing at all in it, I am glad I am not down yonder, where those men are.' Then turning his eyes again upon Hamlet, 'Ay, you may draw your sword; what signifies a sword against the power of the devil?' . . .

"At the end of the play Jones asked Partridge which of the players he had liked best. To this he answered, with some appearance of indignation at the question, 'The king, without doubt.'

" 'Indeed, Mr. Partridge,' says Mrs. Miller. 'You are not of the same opinion with the town; for they are all agreed that Hamlet is acted by the best player who ever was on the stage.'

" 'He the best player!' cried Partridge, with a contemptuous sneer. 'Why, I could act as well as he myself. I am sure, if I had seen a ghost, I should have looked in the very same manner, and done just as he did. And then, to be sure, in that scene, as you called it, between him and his mother, where you told me he acted so fine, why, Lord help me! any man, that is, any good man, that had such a mother, would have done exactly the same. I know you are only joking with me; but indeed, madam, though I was never at a play in London, yet I have seen acting before in the country; and the king for my money: he speaks all his words distinctly, half as loud again as the other. Anybody may see he is an actor.' "

I SUPPOSE Fielding meant this to be a piece of dramatic criticism, which of course it is—a concern with the *how* more than the *what*, an interest in the process, not in the result, coupled with an occasional itch for the *why*. But I am more interested in Partridge than I am in Garrick.

Did Tom Jones enjoy the play more or less than Partridge? This is the crucial, but it is a foolishly quantitative, question. Let me rephrase it.

Did Partridge's dramatically induced belief in the ghost give him more—no, an extra fillip of—enjoyment, which Tom's critical faculties denied him? His enjoyment of them would exclude all belief in a ghost as anything but a dramatic device.

Is there a special kind of belief—call it what you choose, poetical, dramatic, aesthetic—without which we should leave off being spectators and be-

12

come critics, and art, all art, would wither on the stalk of criticism?

There has been a good deal of speculation about such belief. Coleridge, I think, opened it with his arresting, and at the same time confusing, reference to "That willing suspension of disbelief for the moment, which constitutes poetic faith."

I. A. Richards says that Coleridge put it "not quite in the happiest terms, for we are neither aware of a disbelief nor voluntarily suspending it in these cases."

As to being aware or unaware of disbelief, the confusion, my confusion, is rinsed clean, for me, by the thought that there is no such thing as disbelief; except for nonsense, which we cherish for the very reason that we can't believe it. There is no other disbelief.

Disbelief is only the attitude we take toward something that strikes us as irreconcilable with what we already believe. There is a long spectrum of varying degrees and differing kinds of belief. At one end, there is the belief that is vouchsafed to some, a total belief that there are things that are true and real. At the other end, there is not disbelief but a believing in things *as if* they were so.

❋ 7 ❋

"It is doubtless of great moment that an advocate should appear to believe in his case, as he is then more likely to convince others; but I think that most Counsel would be better advocates did they content themselves with simulating the belief instead of actually embracing it. The manifest appearance of a believer is all that is wanted; and this can well be acted after a little study, and will not interfere with that calmness of judgment which it is well to preserve in the midst of uncertainties, and which does not appear to be consistent with much faith."

THERE'S NOT so much difference as you may think between simulating a belief, as Mr. Justice Darling advises an advocate to do, and the willing suspension of disbelief that Coleridge recommends to the reader of poetry. A reader is concerned only with himself. The advocate is pleading for the belief in question, and I have never yet known anyone who could speak very long in favor of something without taking his tongue out of his cheek.

❋ 8 ❋

"Hypocrisy is the homage vice pays to virtue."

I HAVE NO doubt La Rochefoucauld would instantly agree that likewise fraud is the homage force pays to reason, for he was as rational as he was egoistic.

❋ 9 ❋

"Honesty is the best policy."

WHY DO WE never follow this up with Archbishop Whately's comment that "he who is governed by that maxim is not an honest man"? It is to be indifferently honest, honest only as this world goes.

How much more moral are the words of Shakespear's Autolycus! "Ha, ha! What a fool Honesty is! And Trust, his sworn brother, a very simple gentleman!"

About this brother Trust, Henry L. Stimson, in a memorandum to President Roosevelt in September 1945, said, "The chief lesson I have learned in a long life is that the only way you can make a man trustworthy is to trust him; and the surest way to make him untrustworthy is to distrust him and show your distrust."

❋ 10 ❋

"I never heard of any real authority for any such proposition as that one owes full disclosure of the truth to all men at all times."

POLLOCK, YOU WILL note, does not condone a falsification, but only less than the whole truth.

❃ 11 ❃

Holmes, in one of his letters to Laski, speaks of
"the saying that a Frenchman wouldn't mind lying
about facts on occasion but would think himself
dishonored if untrue to his beliefs—whereas an Eng-
lishman who wouldn't misstate facts would equivo-
cate about his beliefs. I suspect there is truth in it
and that it points to the French being on a higher
plane quoad hoc."

AND HERE, you will note, Holmes is only prefer-
ring one to the other.

❃ 12 ❃

"The reason why we hate a liar is not the immoral-
ity, but his gall, thinking we'd believe him."

I THINK I could pass this off as Mark Twain—that
is, as something out of Pudd'nhead Wilson's
Calendar.

17

Have you ever found yourself very angry, a little more angry than you'd expected, when someone lied to you? Not all of your anger was indignation at his lack of veracity. You were angered at his rudeness. For his lie carried with it not only a falsehood, but a belief that you were a fool, stupid enough to be deceived. He was rude, and you had a right to be angry as well as indignant.

❀ 13 ❀

"I say and pray ye speak wel by the law til I next meet with you, though it appear by my letter, that conscience and the law stand subcontrary in figura. The reason of that craveth a quire of paper at the least. I leave it therefore for a further leisure."

I'M NOT QUITE sure I even yet know just what this phrase, "subcontrary *in figura*," means. Subcontraries are things that agree in quantity but differ in quality. The more there is of one attribute or component, the less there is of another. So a law may be more, or less, a matter of conscience.

But the phrase *in figura*? I think this means no more than "in their configuration," "taking both conscience and the law together as a unit." But it certainly sounds as if there were more to it than that. I will ask Franklin Parker, who gave me the quotation.

❋ 14 ❋

". . . and no amount of eloquence will make an English lawyer think that loyalty to truth should come before loyalty to his client."

So SAID Mr. Furnival, the barrister who defended Lady Mason at her trial in Trollope's *Orley Farm*.

❋ 15 ❋

"Dr. Johnson observed that 'he did not care to speak ill of any man behind his back, but he believed the gentleman was an attorney.'"

I THINK we could have persuaded Dr. Johnson that lawyers held at least one virtue in higher esteem and exercised it to better account than the

19

run of mankind. This is the virtue of loyalty and devotion to the interests of another.

"Yes," Dr. Johnson would have retorted. "Lawyers have the virtue of loyalty toward their clients. It gives them high standards of ethics and morality toward their clients, but toward the rest of mankind, sir, by so much are their standards the lower and the meaner. If a man draws the line between right and wrong higher up on the blackboard of his conscience for some than for all, it must be lower for the others."

Is this a great blunt truth? Or is it simply the definition that Polemarchos gives Socrates at the beginning of the *Republic*, that justice is no more than giving every man what you owe him, good to your friends, evil to your enemies? It may be, but you and I are not going to get to the bottom of justice tonight.

The important thing is to distinguish sharply between altruistic and vicarious conduct. The beau ideal of the altruist is a benevolent despotism. His moral risk is the corruption of power, against which benevolence offers no immunity and scarcely any security.

The vicarian, on the other hand, the man who acts for another in his stead rather than for his good, is drawn toward his exaggeration in a different direction. I think the vicarian lacks the enthusiasm of the altruist, but what he may lack in zeal he makes up in devotion. His moral risks spring from a tendency to identify himself with the other, with his interests, his plans, his causes; and from the difficulty, in consequence, of remaining fully himself. The more devoted and loyal the vicarian is, and the further he advances in his special and peculiar virtues, by so much the more he hazards his own interests, his own beliefs, his own ideals. He becomes the less himself. He stakes his personality.

This may be all very well. It may be all to the good. It may be for the best. It could be. There are many of us who have been lifted up by those we have worked for. But it may be not. You are serving, almost always, only one aspect, or purpose, or function of your principal. It may be one of his nobler. Yet it may not be noble.

Hence the curious result that a man who acts for another will almost always act either better or worse than either he or the other will himself behave for his own account.

❈ 16 ❈

"Mr. Glacier met Roger and Mr. Plumb in the Law Courts and thanked them for their help. 'But what a lot of time and money,' he said, 'it has cost to arrive at the truth.'

" 'The truth?' said Roger. 'No one in Court said anything about arriving at the truth.' "

Do you know Roger Thursby? He is the barrister in those two novels of Henry Cecil, *Brothers in Law* and *Friends at Court*. Mr. Glacier is the owner and proprietor of the Glorious Hotel, and Roger has just succeeded in getting him off a charge of bribing two policemen.

I'm afraid that some will take Roger Thursby's reply as somewhat cynical. Not so. He is much too intelligent a lawyer for such a thought, though he may very well have expected his client, Mr. Glacier, to take it so.

"It is not to be forgotten," Edmund M. Morgan said, "that a law suit is not a scientific investigation for the discovery of truth, but a proceeding to determine the basis for, and to arrive at a settlement of, a dispute between litigants." And in his

22

Carpentier Lectures at Columbia, Morgan defined a trial as "a proceeding not for the discovery of truth as such, but for the establishment of a basis of fact for the adjustment of a dispute between litigants. Still it must never be forgotten that its prime objective is to have that basis as close an approximation to the truth as is practicable."

This is enough to show that Thursby was not speaking cynically. I rather think he would go further and agree with me that truth, that is, the true facts, is only an ingredient of justice, which is something larger than truth and far more difficult to attain. In justice we are dealing, not just with events, or facts, or circumstances, or conduct, or behavior, or acts, but with human satisfactions: the satisfactions of the litigants, of their friends and families and associates, and others less directly or more contingently concerned, those who already are or sometime may be in a like predicament. Indeed, you might say that justice is composed chiefly of the satisfaction of everybody even remotely concerned in the case—except the lawyers and the judge.

❋ 17 ❋

"How odd it is," Darwin said, *"that anyone should not see that all observation must be for or against some view if it is to be of any service!"*

THIS, YOU WILL in turn observe, was said by one of the greatest scientific observers of all, Charles Darwin. I am a lawyer, and when I read this, my legal heart leaped up. A great scientist praises the art of advocacy! The Royal Society merges with the Inns of Court! The American Academy of Arts and Sciences amalgamates with the American Bar Association! All I can say is in extenuation of my first enthusiasm.

Whitehead told Lucien Price that most propositions were half-truths. "Under one aspect it may be false; and under another, true. Whether it is true or false will depend upon its relevancy. In the aspect in which it is relevant we call it true, and in the aspect in which it is irrelevant, untrue. Actually it is neither, and it is both, depending upon the relevancy in which it is seen. A half-truth, you see. And it is taking these half-truths for whole truths that raises the mischief."

Darwin's "view" is, of course, the same as Whitehead's "aspect." Whether it is "for or against," in Darwin's words, is the same as Whitehead's relevancy, that is, whether it is toward the purpose in hand. Both agree that you have to set out to go somewhere if you want to get anywhere. Impartiality is nothing more than a vacancy of mind. In its purest state, it is either ignorance or idiocy. For a lawyer, it is the state of his mind before a client comes into his office. For a scientist, it is the appropriate attitude before he poses the problem. But not for long for either. Almost immediately they take sides.

Yet there is a difference. The advocate is committed. He is engaged. He is retained by his client. The scientist, on the other hand, takes sides only tentatively. He is free to change sides, as the lawyer is not. The scientist zigzags his way toward the truth. He is the admirable renegade. The lawyer is a continual convert.

❋ 18 ❋

"The opening of the atomic age may well mark the end of the first chapter of the physical sciences and our partial mastery of our physical environment. It is conventional to ascribe this mastery to the development of scientific method, and there has been much discussion of what the essence of the scientific method is. It appears to me, however, that it is easy to take too narrow a view in this matter. I like to say that there is no scientific method as such, but that the most vital feature of the scientist's procedure has been merely to do his utmost with his mind, no holds barred. This means in particular that no special privileges are accorded to authority or to tradition, that personal prejudices and predilections are carefully guarded against, that one makes continued check to assure oneself that one is not making mistakes, and that any line of inquiry will be followed that appears at all promising. All of these rules are applicable to any situation in which one has to obtain the right answer and all of them are only manifestations of intelligence. The so-called scientific method is merely a special case of the method of intelligence, and any apparently unique characteristics are to be explained by the *nature of the subject matter rather than* ascribed to the nature of the method itself."

IF A SCIENTIST had clients to serve and rules to follow, the scientific truths he pursues would turn out to be more just than true. If a lawyer were to owe no duty to his clients and if he were free to do his damnedest to find the truth, what he found would be the more true and the less just.

But the lawyer works under rules as strict as those prescribed by Hoyle. Justice Holmes used to speak of justice in a somewhat disconcerting way, and when he did he would say very much what he wrote to my mother, on December 14, 1919. "As to the love of justice I can't help chuckling. As I am in the habit of saying to my brethren, I hate justice, meaning thereby that when I hear a man appealing to that I expect to find it an apology for not playing the game according to the rules—dodging some settled principle without articulate discrimination."

The difference between scientific methods and legal procedure lies in the difference between truth and justice. If they were one and the same thing, we could not have both.

❊ 19 ❊

"Desire to know why, and how, curiosity, which is a lust of the mind, that by a perseverance of delight in the continued and indefatigable generation of knowledge, exceedeth the short vehemence of any carnal pleasure."

H OBBES, I THINK, was here seizing happily on an analogy that was a commonplace in the pulpit. For the O.E.D. tells me that a Puritan divine named Thomas Brooks, in 1675, in a book with the promising title, *A Golden Key to Open Hidden Treasure*, called curiosity "the spiritual adultery of the soul."

Montaigne, certainly one of the most inquisitive of men, in much the same spirit as Hobbes, had inscribed on the wall of his library, "*Cognoscendi studium homini dedit Deus eius torquendi gratia*"; and he put it into one of his *Essays*, "*La curiosité de connoistre les choses esté donnée aux hommes pour fleau, dit la sacrosainte parole*." God made man inquisitive to torture him.

Pascal, I think, had Montaigne in the back of his mind, as he so often had, when he said, "When we do not know the truth about something it is well that there should be a common error which fixes men's minds as, for example, the moon, to which is attributed the changes of the seasons, the progress of diseases, etc. For the chief malady of mankind is a restless curiosity about things he cannot know; and it is not so bad for him to be in error as it is to be curious to no purpose."

Pascal was thinking of the truth that is revealed to us. This is not the attitude to take toward the truths we discover for ourselves. Schrödinger says, "In an honest search for knowledge you quite often have to abide by ignorance for an indefinite period. Instead of filling a gap by guesswork, genuine science prefers to put up with it; and this, not so much from conscientious scruples about telling lies, as from the consideration that, however irksome the gap may be, its obliteration by a fake removes the urge to seek after a tenable answer. So efficiently may attention be diverted that the answer is missed even when, by good luck, it comes close at hand. The steadfastness in standing up to a *non liquet*, nay in appreciating it as a stimulus and a signpost to further quest, is a natural and indispensable disposition in the mind of a scientist."

Oppenheimer concisely summed it up with the remark: "It is the business of science to be wrong."

❊ 20 ❊

"_. . . in her strong toil of grace . . ._"

IF I COULD read this phrase sensibly, it would not interest me the way it does. To me the phrase means an exertion of strength, gracefully and elegantly made. To me the words "strong toil" mean a great effort of strength.

In the context, of course, they do not mean this at all. In the final scene of Shakespear's _Antony and Cleopatra_, Caesar Augustus is looking down at the dead body of Cleopatra, and he remarks, "She looks like sleep, as she would catch another Antony in her strong toil of grace." Toil is obviously a net. But not to me. I can't help reading the phrase my own way, and I see no reason why I shouldn't.

I. A. Richards was struck by this phrase, and in his _Philosophy of Rhetoric_ says, "Where, in terms of what entries in what possible dictionary do the meanings here of _toil_ and _grace_ come to rest?"

We associate grace, as we do elegance, with beauty. We think of the grace in the movements of a dancer, in the carriage of a woman walking, in the curves of lines. We neglect the importance of grace in the exertion of strength. Have you ever seen a champion prizefighter? The champion is as graceful in the ring as Nijinsky ever was in a ballet. Not the second-raters. I think the great quality that makes a champion is grace of movement. It is what chiefly distinguishes him from the others. Jack Johnson, Dempsey, Tunney, Louis, Georges Carpentier, Sugar Ray Robinson. Seeing is believing. I'd not need to say this if you had seen them in slow motion. Watch a pile driver. There is grace in the accelerating fall of the weight. Look at a great building. It can be as massive as you please, and full of grace as well as strength.

❈ 21 ❈

"Take heart of grace."

THE PHRASE RANG in my ears as I walked out in the crowd at the annual dinner of the American Law Institute five years ago. Learned Hand had just finished speaking, and he had ended with these words: "Courage, my friends! Take heart of grace. The devil is not yet dead."

What a phrase! "Take heart of grace." So far as I know it occurs only here and in the song Mabel sings in the first act of Gilbert and Sullivan's *The Pirates of Penzance:*

31

"Poor wand'ring one!
Tho' thou hast surely strayed,
Take heart of grace,
Thy steps retrace,
Poor wand'ring one!
Poor wand'ring one!
If such poor love as mine
Can help thee find
True peace of mind,
Why, take it, it is thine!
Take heart, fair days will shine;
Take any heart—take mine!"

What makes Learned Hand's words memorable is the kind of courage he was calling on, the kind that cannot be confused with optimism. "Take heart of grace. The Devil is *not* yet dead."

❁ 22 ❁

"But that was in another country; and besides, the wench is dead."

IF I WERE blessed with a memory of fornication in another country with a girl who had died, I think I might understand why this sentence has for me a halo of romance. As it is, I can only believe that there is some inexplicable spell in the very words. They are Christopher Marlowe's, in *The Jew of Malta*, and he used them in a scene so far from romantic that I wonder if he was aware of their potency. Barabas, the Jew, is on a street in Malta. With him is his slave, who sees two friars approaching. "Look, look, master, here come two religious caterpillars!" And Barabas says, "I smelt 'em ere they came." The friars abuse him. "Thou hast committed fornication," they say. These magic words are his reply.

I found them first in Ernest Hemingway, who can make magic with the best of them, in his *Across the River and Into the Trees*, in one of the love scenes between the Colonel and Renata, the Italian girl. Renata is asking the Colonel about his wife. He tells her that they have been long separated, and he adds, "But that was in another country, and besides the wench is dead." "Is she really dead?" the girl asks. "Deader than Phoebus the Phoenician," he answers. "But she doesn't know it yet."

T. S. Eliot, too, picked them up, and used them for a headnote to his verses called *Portrait of a Lady*.

Frederic Brown called one of his whodunits *The Wench Is Dead*, and he too used the quotation as a headnote, opposite the copyright page.

I know that a situation or a context can exalt even mean words, rude words, coarse words; and they in return will sometimes point up and firm up what would otherwise be too emotional or too sentimental. But here in Marlowe, Hemingway, Eliot, and Brown the context is either sordid or jocular or deliberately cynical or plainly popular. Yet these words shine with their own interior light, and here are four writers who testify to this truth.

There are other words that move me without my knowing why or how. Do not call them pure poetry, any more than you would praise wine by likening it to distilled water. Pure poetry may be like white light, made up of all the colors, but it seems to me that it is of the very nature of poetry to be impure.

"Give not a windy night a rainy morrow" is to me a piece of magic. It is in the 90th Sonnet, and I give you the four lines:

"Ah, do not, when my heart hath scap'd this sorrow,
Come in the rearward of a conquered woe;
Give not a windy night a rainy morrow,
To linger out a purpos'd overthrow."

I told my wife I liked this, and she said that she liked "A wind rose in the night." I asked her where she had got that, and she did not know. Nor could she tell me why she liked it, except that it was about looking out of a window after someone had died.

Or another verse on defeat, terser but no less talismanic:

34

"He ask'd the way to Chester; and of him
I did demand what news from Shrewsbury.
He told me that rebellion had ill luck,
And that young Harry Percy's spur was cold."

Feel how the pun bites.
Now turn to this:

"Time hath, my lord, a wallet at his back,
Wherein he puts alms for oblivion."

Time, a pilgrim, accepting alms and putting
them in his wallet; and then going on his way, on
his pilgrimage to oblivion. All I know is that these
two lines surely mean more than I understand.

Not all my reverberating lines are so inexplicable. There are these two in Emily Brontë's verse:

"I'll walk where my own nature would be leading.
It vexes me to choose another guide."

This, it seems to me, has quite simply the merit
of a perfect statement, in feeling and tone of voice
as well as in precision. Is it poetry? You can read it
with equal satisfaction as prose. Listen to the
words "vexes" and "choose." To me these two
lines are a good example of the power of language
to transcend both of the two rhetorical categories,
poetry and prose. Emily Brontë, in these two lines,
was writing, not either, but both at once. She

dropped into unmistakably bad poetry in the two that follow:

"Where the grey flocks in ferny glens are feeding,
  Where the wild wind blows on the mountain's
    side."

Turn to ten lines that "snatch a grace beyond the reach of art." No one knows who wrote them. You will find the whole poem in *The Oxford Book of Light Verse*, under the title, "Tom o' Bedlam," and in Walter de la Mare's *Come Hither*.

"With an host of furious fancies,
  Whereof I am commander:
  With a burning spear
  And a horse of air,
  To the wilderness I wander.
  By a knight of ghosts and shadows,
  I summoned am to tourney:
  Ten leagues beyond
  The wild world's end—
  Methinks it is no journey."

❁ 23 ❁

"The waves became his winding sheet;
  The waters were his tomb;
  But for his fame, the ocean sea
  Was not sufficient room."

Of Drake, Sir Francis Drake, who died and was buried at sea, off Porto Bello, in 1596.

Am I wrong in thinking this very good indeed about the man who sacked Cadiz and beat off the Armada?

❁ 24 ❁

"Ripeness is all."

It is equally inexplicable to me how some lines stir others and leave me cold. These three words from *Lear* seemed to T. S. Eliot "to have profound emotional meaning." This is in his little book on

Dante, where he also says that Keats's "Beauty is truth, truth beauty . . ." "seems to me meaningless; or perhaps, the fact that it is grammatically meaningless conceals another meaning from me." Eliot adds that "on rereading the whole *Ode*, this line strikes me as a serious blemish on a beautiful poem; and the reason must be either that I fail to understand it, or that it is a statement which is untrue."

As to this line of Keats, I agree. But the words from *Lear* leave me unstirred, and I don't think it is because I fail to understand them, nor because I do not agree with them. For the same thought does move me as Shakespear expressed it in another and earlier play, *Love's Labour's Lost*.

There Holofernes, who is a schoolmaster, speaking "a leash of languages," and a purposely ridiculous character, says, "This is a gift that I have, simple, simple; a foolish extravagant spirit, full of forms, figures, shapes, objects, ideas, apprehensions, motions, revolutions. These are begot in the ventricle of memory, nourished in the womb of pia mater, and delivered upon the mellowing of occasion."

"The mellowing of occasion." I think this beats "Ripeness is all." I am sure I don't know why, but Shakespear liked it. He used it again in *Twelfth Night*. Viola says, ". . . till I had made mine own occasion mellow."

Shakespear could speak as plainly as he chose, and I think the more seriously, the less metaphorically and the more plainly. Thus Hamlet drops all metaphor when he speaks of his own death. "There's a special providence in the fall of a sparrow. If it be now, 'tis not to come. If it be not to come, it will be now. If it be not now, yet it will come. *The readiness is all.* Since no man has aught of what he leaves, what is't to leave betimes? Let be." And then the King and his Court enter; and go into the final scene.

Goethe remarked once to his friend Chancellor von Müller, "What does a man do, then, of significance, unless he is stirred by some particular occasion? Occasions are the true muses. They shake us out of our dreaming, and we ought to be eternally grateful to them." "All my poems," Goethe told Eckermann, "are occasional verses. They were aroused by reality, and therein they have their ground and their base. Of poems taken out of the air, have I none."

❊ 25 ❊

"The days come and go like muffled and veiled figures sent from a distant friendly party, but they say nothing, and if we do not use the gifts they bring, they carry them as silently away."

TEN YEARS LATER, in the first issue of the *Atlantic Monthly*, in 1857, Emerson turned this journal entry into poetry:

"*Daughters of Time, the hypocritic Days,*
  Muffled and dumb like barefoot dervishes,
  And marching single in an endless file,
  Bring diadems and fagots in their hands.
  To each they offer gifts after his will,
  Bread, kingdoms, stars, and sky that holds them
    all.
  I, in my pleached garden, watched the pomp,
  Forgot my morning wishes, hastily
  Took a few herbs and apples, and the Day
  Turned and departed silent. I, too late,
  Under her solemn fillet saw the scorn."

There are none of the trappings of poetry in these stanzas. They do not announce themselves as poetry. They just are poetry. I am sorry only that Emerson dropped the "distant friendly party." It does not fit, but it suggests somehow that Father Time is domiciled in a pleasant friendly sort of small town, something like Concord.

❋ 26 ❋

"Is there any room at your head, Saunders?
Is there any room at your feet?
Is there any room at your side, Saunders,
Where fain, fain, I would sleep?"

IN THE MARGIN of this Scotch ballad my mother wrote: "Oh, churl, drunk all? And left no friendly drop To help me after?"

You will recall that Juliet added, leaning over Romeo,

"I will kiss thy lips.
Haply some poison yet doth hang on them,
To make me die with a restorative.
Thy lips are warm."

❋ 27 ❋

"Out of the old fields cometh the new corn."

Aⁿ ᵁᴺᴱˣᴾᴱᶜᵀᴱᴰ remark to find its way out of
Chaucer into Coke's *Fourth Institute*.

I do not see why we are so squeamish about
plagiarism. I don't mean the infringement of copyright. I mean taking and using what is in the public domain. "For such kind of borrowing as this, if
it be not bettered by the borrower, among good authors is accounted plagiary," said Milton.

But only "if it be not bettered by the borrower."

Listen to what Shakespear can do, and in *Antony
and Cleopatra* did do, to a passage he'd been reading in North's translation of Plutarch:

"I will tell you," Enobarbus said.
"The barge she sat in, like a burnish'd throne,
  Burn'd on the water. The poop was beaten gold;
  Purple the sails, and so perfumed that
  The winds were lovesick with them; the oars were
    silver,
  Which to the tune of flutes kept stroke, and made
  The water which they beat to follow faster,

42

As amorous of their strokes. For her own person,
It beggar'd all description.
She did lie in her pavilion, cloth-of-gold, of tissue,
O'erpicturing that Venus where we see
The fancy outwork nature. On each side her
Stood pretty dimpled boys, like smiling Cupids,
With divers-color'd fans, whose wind did seem
To glow the delicate cheeks which they did cool,
And what they undid, did.
Her gentlewomen, like the Nereides,
So many mermaids, tended her in the eyes,
And made their bends adornings. At the helm
A seeming mermaid steers. The silken tackle
Swell with the touches of those flower-soft hands
That yarely frame the office. From the barge
A strange invisible perfume hits the sense
Of the adjacent wharfs. The city cast
Her people out upon her; and Antony,
Enthron'd in the market place, did sit alone,
Whistling to the air, which, but for vacancy,
Had gone to gaze on Cleopatra too,
And made a gap in nature."

T. S. Eliot said—and I take it from Theodore
Spencer's introduction to the play, "Immature
poets imitate; mature poets steal." Shakespear
stole this from North's Plutarch, which had been
published a dozen years before.

"So, she furnished herselfe with a world of gifts,
store of gold and silver, and of riches and other
sumptuous ornaments, as is credible enough she

43

might bring from so great a house, and from so wealthie and rich a realme as AEgypt was. But yet she caried nothing with her wherein she trusted more than in her selfe, and in the charmes and inchauntment of her passing beautie and grace.

"Therefore when she was sent unto by diuers letters, both from *Antonius* himselfe, and also from his friendes, she made so light of it and mocked *Antonius* so much, that she disdained to set forward otherwise, but to take her barge in the river of Cydnus, the poop whereof was of gold, the sailes of purple, and the owers of silver, which kept stroke in rowing after the sound of the musicke of flutes, howboyes, cytherns, vyolls, and such other instruments as they played upon in the barge.

"And now for the person of her selfe: She was laide under a pavillion of cloth of golde of tissue, apparelled and attired like the goddesse *Venus*, commonly drawen in picture: and hard by her, on either hand of her, pretie faire boyes apparelled as painters doe set foorth god *Cupide*, with litle fans in their hands, with the which they fanned winde upon her.

"Her ladies and gentlewomen also, the fairest of them were apparelled like the nymphes *Nereides* (which are the myrmaides of the waters) and like the *Graces*, some stearing the helme, others tending the tackle and ropes of the barge, out of the which there came a wonderfull passing sweete savor of perfumes, that perfumed the wharfes side, pestered with innumerable multitudes of people.

44

"Some of them followed the barge all alongst the rivers side: others also ranne out of the citie to see her comming in. So that in the end, there ranne such multitudes of people one after an other to see her, that *Antonius* was left post alone in the market place, in his Imperiall seate to give audience: and there went a rumor in the peoples mouthes, that the goddesse *Venus* was come to play with the god *Bacchus*, for the generall good of all Asia."

❋ 28 ❋

"Granted, that to judge a man it may be necessary to pass in review both his work and his life. It is not necessary to review his life in order to judge his work. Every work should be considered independently of its author, as something anonymous, or as a fragment of a fresco one sees retrieved from a catacomb. Then, and then only, is it possible to know passionately what the man was like."

WE KNOW nothing about Homer, not even whether there ever was such a person, little about Socrates, nothing much about Plato, aside from what one said and the other wrote. Likewise with the other great writers of ancient Greece. Antiquity had its own ideas about biography.

We know little about Shakespear the man, nothing about what Dante was doing while he was writing *The Divine Comedy*. We do not admire either the plays or the poem any the less for knowing so little about their creators; nor think the more of what Goethe wrote or Victor Hugo wrote for knowing so much about their private lives.

I think the repeated attacks on Shakespear's authorship of the Plays prove this point. They don't really care who wrote them. For their argument is always that Shakespear couldn't have, and that someone else must have, only because he could have. Enough candidates have been put up to make the author almost anonymous.

The man is one thing. His work is another. So far as we are concerned, they are two separate things. We may be interested in either, but it is imprudent of us to bring them together, unless the author himself asks us to do so, as, for example, Montaigne did. "I am myself the subject of this book," he said.

❋ 29 ❋

"Many books require no thought from those who read them, and for a very simple reason;—they made no such demand upon those who wrote them."

M AX, YOU WILL recognize your friend, the Reverend Charles Caleb Colton, the man who attracted your attention when he said there were three difficulties in authorship: "to write anything worth the publishing; to find honest men to publish it; and to get sensible men to read it." I don't know how you found his book, *Lacon*, but as one aphoriphile to another I congratulate you; and as to these difficulties, there are not many who have done more to make them less.

What Colton says is very true, and authors as well as readers find it a great blessing, this relief from thought. And why not? There must be as many kinds of books as there are kinds of readers. After all, the best books are the most readable. What else are books for? I'd rather read the menu or the label on a bottle than stare at the tablecloth, or read *Paradise Lost* or *The Faery Queene* or *The Testament of Beauty* than not read anything.

But what Colton says ceases to be true of books that call for any thought. With them, the more thought they require of the reader, the greater by many times is the demand they make on the writer. The more pains he takes, the less he puts the reader to, and by a fantastic ratio. I don't know how much rewriting, how many hours of rethinking and rephrasing, a writer must spend simply to save the reader trouble. The author is like the host at a party. It is his party, but he must not enjoy himself so much that he neglects his guests. His enjoyment is not so much his own as it is theirs.

❊ 30 ❊

"Round numbers are always false."

DOCTOR JOHNSON's round statement is as false as any round number.

The truth is, round numbers on many occasions are more truthful than precise numbers. A short, say a six-inch, slide rule will give you a more candid answer than a longer one, when the factors are known to no more significant figures than the rule can handle. Beyond that, any answer is fanciful and deceptive. For to make your answer more precise than your data is to give it a false face. A fair curve is a matter of veracity as well as beauty.

It depends on what you are dealing with. If you are figuring the cost of the hundred shares of stock you have bought, you can truthfully carry out the result to cents. If you are figuring how much those shares will earn the nearest dime is probably as near as you can hope to get to the truth.

I remember the way we were marked in school. The monthly averages were read out to a silent assembly of all the boys, and thereby we were ranked. Each boy's average was carried out to three significant figures: 6.58, let us say, if you barely passed; 7.77 would be pretty good; 8.58, say, might mean you led your form. Three significant figures, and the third was as significant as the first two. Indeed it was decisive, because it would put you ahead or behind the next boy. To what folly an insistence on ranking us had to stoop!

It was gratifying to read what Mr. B. C. Brookes told the Mathematical Association in England recently:

"When I was a schoolmaster," Mr. Brookes confided, "we took marks from all kinds of sources, added them, averaged them, arranged them in order, and gave the boy who got the highest score the form prize or a scholarship. A boy who got 73 per cent, was better than a boy who got 72 per cent—in fact about 1.4 per cent better—and parents and headmasters were distressed if a boy's geography mark dropped from 50 per cent in one term to 49 per cent in the next. Indeed, the only point at is-sue was the cause of this decline—was it a waning of intellectual ability or a weakening of moral fibre? The mark itself must never be questioned once it appeared on the official form!"

I am surprised that Doctor Johnson did not per-ceive that these round numbers were no falser than abstractions. They are, indeed, abstractions. For they differ from numbers that are less round only in their neglect of an irrelevant precision, a degree of precision that was not needed for the purpose in hand, and that might be confusing or even mislead-ing.

❋ 31 ❋

"Here in the skirts of the forest, like fringe upon a petticoat."

IT IS A far journey from the Forest of Arden to what I want to say, but Rosalind's conceit is my metaphor, as I hope to make clear.

I will begin with a quotation from Quine:

"Perhaps, indeed, the best treatment of the mat-ter will prove to consist in abandoning all notion of so-called meanings as entities; thus such phrases as 'having *meaning*' and 'same *in meaning*' might be dropped in favor of '*significant*' and '*synonymous*,' in hopes eventually of devising adequate criteria of significance and synonymy involving no excursion through a realm of intermediary entities called meanings."

About synonymy I have nothing to say, because I don't believe there is any. I cannot see any synonyms unless I restrict meaning to the narrow sector which is the relation of the word to what it refers to. Then I am ignoring its relation to the writer and its relation to the reader. If I take these into account, I doubt if there are as many synonyms in the language of a country as there are identical twins among its people. Words are no more alike than people. A word can be translated out of one language into another, just as a citizen of one country can be naturalized into another, but in neither case is more than the nationality changed, not the individuality.

What is in my mind is Quine's suggestion that we drop the word *meaning* in favor of *significance*. I suppose he is taking significance in its sense of importance. Otherwise we should find ourselves back where we started, with nothing more useful than a fresh word. A word's significance, then, is the part it plays in the situation or scene in which it makes its appearance. Its significance is no different in kind from the significance of anything else in the situation, everything that attracts our attention and our consideration.

The words you speak are just another item contributing to my understanding of the whole, which may be more words. Then we call them the context. But there are also the circumstances, the clothes you are wearing, your posture, your gestures, your tone of voice, the chair you are sitting in or the lectern you are holding with both hands, the rest of the furniture in the room, the color of the wallpaper, and the other people who are listening—they all are important in their several and distinct capacities and degrees. The words are as much a part of the picture as they are in a comic strip where they are put into a balloon coming out of their speaker's mouth.

I don't know how far the adoption of "significance" instead of "meaning" will take us, but clearly, as Quine says, it has the great merit of ridding us of the delusion that there are such things, such separate entities, as meanings. For significance is clearly a matter of degree, an affair of more or less importance.

So far, so good. But there is, I think, a class of words whose significance is better understood if they are treated differently. These are words that are intended to be applied to future action, words of command, advice, request, expectation, agreement, and so forth. Statutes, contracts, and wills are good and obvious examples, but this class of words goes far beyond the law.

The reason why these words, and such words as these, are better treated as a class apart is that they are so seldom part of a situation. As time passes, they are left to go more and more on their own. When the time comes to match them against the conduct or the event or the act to which they were intended to be applied, the scene has darkened or the curtain has fallen. These words, like actors and actresses after the play is over, have taken off their costumes. They are no longer characters, but people. To drop the metaphor, these words have to carry their own significance as best they can.

This is a difficult thing for them to do. A word quite out of context has almost no significance. A dictionary tells us as little about a word as Who's Who tells us about a man. The larger the context, from sentence to paragraph, and on from there to all that was said, and beyond that to a reconstruction of the circumstances, by so much the better do we know the scope of a word. But now, when time has stripped it of all but its immediate context, darkened its background, and blurred its circumstances, its significance lies in its application to new actions and events that did not exist when it was uttered. This is its significance, and it is all the significance it has. It is almost a stranger, a traveler from an antique land.

The one important characteristic of such words so used is extension. Their only significance lies in the extent of their generality.

There are some words of which this is not true at all, though they look to the future and are intended to apply to things in the future. These are names and the other words which apply, if they apply to anything, to some particular person or thing. I am not sure they have the right to the dignity of words, for they simply point. They are only a fore-finger of a word.

Putting names to one side, the great virtue of the words I am talking about lies in the extent and scope of their vagueness. Their significance is a matter of the extent of their aura or of their penumbra. You may look at it either way, light or shadow.

In their aura or penumbra lies their virtue, and their writer or their speaker exploits this virtue by selecting words and phrases of just the right amount of vagueness, that is, the precise degree of imprecision that he wants, so as to give the appropriate scope and tether of discretion he wants or expects their recipient to exercise in the future. He pays out their significance. The more he thinks he knows what the future will bring, or the less confidence he has in the recipient's later or superior sagacity, the more careful he will be to choose specific and definite words. The less he knows about the future, and the more trust he has in the recipient, the more scope he will pay out, and the vaguer, or the more elastic, will be the words and phrases he will choose. The recipient knows what is going on. He will stretch the elasticity of the words, he will move about within their vagueness, he will stretch them, he will tug at the tether, so that he and they together may best meet the occasion which they are jointly expected to handle. It is a joint enterprise.

The significance of such words as these, words used to restrict or control action in the future, lies in the degree of their generality or particularity. This is a simple enough virtue, but we must not fail to recognize its power. The mass of the multitude of more or less specific provisions in our laws, in the contracts we sign and the agreements we make, the wills we leave, the plans we propose, and even the wishes and hopes we express, are all pressing the past upon our present and our present upon the future. We are caught and held in a vast reticulation. Our yesterdays have been imposed upon us, and we retaliate by trying to make our own tomorrows.

❊ 32 ❊

"The glittering and sounding generalities of natural right which make up the Declaration of Independence."

WHEN EMERSON was told that Rufus Choate had said this, Emerson exclaimed, "Glittering generalities! They are blazing ubiquities!"

Whether they glitter or they blaze, large generalities do not burn with their own flame. They reflect the fire in the speaker, who is using them to express himself and not anything else.

This is more true of abstractions. A generality may sometimes serve as a handy compendium of a number of particulars, but an abstraction can express only an attitude.

❋ 33 ❋

"What do we mean when we say that a person has depth? We know what we mean but can't put it into words," Lucien Price asked Whitehead. "Precisely not," he replied, "for depth is the power to take into account all those factors in a situation which cannot be adequately verbalized."

WE MAY, I think, go further. There is also depth below what a man could but doesn't say, in what he chooses not to say, prefers to leave unsaid, and in what he does not think there is any need of saying.

What a man can say, what he can "verbalize," shows only the surface of his thought. The point I want to make is that we can see a little below the surface, if we get the light right, and I don't think it much matters to us whether he cannot or just doesn't adequately verbalize it.

Everything anyone says implies something more than it states. Everything you say is a quotation out of a text, a line or so and a couple of bars from a song, a passage from a book. The best talent can imply the most. A great actress once boasted she could portray any emotion from the wings, showing only one foot and her arm to the elbow. The deeper the pool of traditions and assumptions she and her audience, like authors and their readers, have in common, the easier it is and the more she can imply. So much so, sometimes, that both take their common understanding as a matter of course and are quite unaware how nearly completely they do indeed understand one another.

Where an inquiry into what may be implied will serve us best is, I think, the implied reference to a standard, the zero point by which we must measure the most straightforward statement. Take this word, *best*. Better can be better than best, and good can be better than better. "The best I can do . . ." How good is your best? I may be able to do better. How do I know? How, to be sure, do you know? What is your boiling point? Fahrenheit or Centigrade? 212° or 100°? Which are you talking? There is a zero implied in any relative statement.

Suppose you are the head of a school recommending one of your students for admission to a college. Every adjective you use about him impliedly refers to the zero point of the standard of your school just as truly as every grade you have given him. Otherwise your words would be no more than exclamations. The Admissions Committee of the college will examine your standard and the position of its zero point in order to understand your student's grades or whatever you have said about him, then they will correct your standard in the light of their experience with your previous recommendations. Finally they will adjust your zero point to their own. It is a transaction in intellectual foreign exchange.

I had an uncle to whom I owe much and from whom I learned much. He was fanatically averse to President Wilson, as later there were those who "hated" President Franklin Roosevelt. My uncle used to refer to President Wilson, inappropriately as well as improperly, as "that son of a bitch in the White House," until one Sunday morning at Nahant, when my uncle announced, "I have ceased calling President Wilson a son of a bitch, out of respect to those I have heretofore designated by that term."

Two years ago at dinner in New York, the talk turned to the initiative taken by the young director of RIAS, the West Berlin Radio, in the riots in East Berlin. Admiration was expressed, except by one man, a distinguished public servant. He thought the young director had done no more than his job demanded of him. I left the dinner disappointed by this comment, and my disappointment lasted until I thought it over. It was a higher compliment to the young director than my admiration. My admiration seemed higher than his, only because my standard of public service was lower than his.

"Above and beyond the call of duty" is relative to the pitch of duty. The lower it is pitched, the higher you appraise the conduct, in depreciated units of praise.

Two men may entirely agree and yet come out with different expressions of opinion.

❄ 34 ❄

ANT: *I'll leave you, lady.*
CLEO: *Courteous lord, one word.*
Sir, you and I must part—but that's not it.
Sir, you and I have lov'd—but there's not it.
That you know well. Something it is I would—
O, my oblivion is a very Antony,
And I am all forgotten!
ANT: *But that your royalty*
Holds idleness your subject, I should take you
For idleness itself.
CLEO: *'Tis sweating labour*
To bear such idleness so near the heart
As Cleopatra this. But, sir, forgive me;
Since my becomings kill me when they do not
Eye well to you. Your honour calls you hence;
Therefore be deaf to my unpitied folly,
And all the gods go with you! Upon your sword
Sit laurel victory, and smooth success
Be strew'd before your feet!

AMBIGUOUS. Antony is leaving for Rome. I wonder if, on his long journey back, it did not occur to him that she might mean she was pregnant.

❊ 35 ❊

"He is skilfull in Rhetorick, which gives a speech
colour, as Logick doth favour, and both together
beauty. Though some condemne Rhetorick as the
mother of lies, speaking more than the truth in
Hyperboles, lesse in her miosis, otherwise in her
metaphors, contrary in her ironies; yet is there excellent use of all these, when disposed of with judgement."

WE SAY MORE than we mean. We say less than
we mean. We say something quite different
from what we mean. And what's more, there is
even a perverse efficacy of understanding in saying
just the contrary of what we mean.

I do these things, not to be obscure or to conceal
what I mean, nor to be euphemistical; but quite
simply because I think it will help you to understand what I mean. By indirections, I find directions out.

When I measure my words to what I am talking
about, saying no more and no less nor otherwise
than whatever that may be, I forego my relation
with you. I am trying to make impersonal what is

necessarily and essentially personal. It's an artificial insemination of meaning.

Take saying more than I mean, exaggerating, using superlatives and hyperboles. It is a rude thing to do, unless I am joking. For it implies that I think you are gullible, or stupid enough not to discount what I say. Like lies, they are insults whenever they imply that you are stupid enough to believe them. They are insolent. At best, an overstatement implies that your standards are lower than mine. If my hyperboles are not affronts to your intelligence, at least they disparage your standards. They mean that I think your moral or your aesthetic values are inflated, cheaper than mine, and so I must raise the price of my remarks.

Understatements are deflations, and so they enhance the value of your units of appreciation. They are, therefore, compliments, for I am deflating my dollars of judgment to make each as valuable as yours.

What interests me is irony, where the statement of the contrary emphasizes the assertion. If there is an air of companionship between the author and the reader, or between the speaker and the listener, in an understatement, then irony, the statement of the contrary of what you mean, brings them into what is really a whispered conspiracy, an understanding to the verge of intimacy. This is a large part of the success of *Tom Jones*. It is a good bit of the delight we take in Jane Austen. Irony runs across their phrases like footsteps across the floor above, or like catspaws of wind across a bay.

❋ 36 ❋

"When you read too fast or too slowly, you do not understand."

THIS THOUGHT turns up twice in the manuscript of Pascal's *Pensées*.

There are books that ask to be read fast. Few detective stories ask the reader for more than two or three sittings and they are better read in one. A good story sets its own pace, and the good reader must keep up. For it is designed and built to move swiftly through its own sparkling chronometrical waters. But most books do not set their own pace. The reader must set his own, from so fast that he is skipping to so slowly that he would do better to re-read each paragraph.

The only drawback to reading slowly is the danger of reading word by word and not sentence by sentence. The sentence is the unit of thought, and a period ought to end a thought. A word is pretty nearly meaningless if you take it alone, and to understand a long or a difficult sentence word by word is quite a feat. This is the only reason why it is inadvisable to follow the words with your finger. It is also why I dislike double columns on the page of a book. They break up a sentence into shorter lengths than when it runs all the way across the page.

❋ 37 ❋

"I think poetry should surprise by a fine excess and not by singularity—it should strike the reader as a wording of his own highest thoughts, and appear almost a remembrance."

KEATS WROTE this to John Taylor on February 27, 1818, and it is so well known that we read it too fast, and it is so beautifully said that we are likely to neglect its precision of statement.

It must be "a *fine* excess." We must be only a little surprised. If we are more than a little surprised, not only do we not understand, but we do not like it. We are offended in our self-esteem at not understanding what is offered us, and in the poise of what we think we already understand.

And it must be "*almost* a remembrance." My brother used to put it too bluntly, when he said that he liked to recognize things. Better to say that it should be a metempsychosis from one of our own former selves, intimations of our own recurrent mortality.

When I apply this admirably precise, this operationally accurate statement of the functions of poetry to my own embarrassment at modern verse and modern art, I feel much better. For then I know that my embarrassment may not be due wholly to stupidity, but may be due to my too short acquaintance with them. I am too surprised. Or else, and perhaps this is the more likely, the poet is talking, not to me, but to someone else.

❋ 38 ❋

"Me imperturbe, *standing at ease in Nature*."

Don't we sometimes underestimate or even ignore the power of inelegant language? Can you write worse and say more than Walt Whitman does here? This word *imperturbe* is not even French, so far as I know. There's no excuse for it, except its impact on our understanding.

Did Thoreau say any more in those two lovely sentences of his? "Though the speech of the poet goes to the heart of things, yet he is that one especially who speaks civilly to Nature as a second person and in some sense is the patron of the world. Though more than any he stands in the midst of Nature, yet more than any he can stand aloof from her."

❋ 39 ❋

"Father, forgive them, for they know not what they do."

HOLMES WROTE Laski that this was "the biggest thing in antiquity." Holmes said it "beats all the classics." What he admired was Jesus' "skeptic tolerance" in "the most dramatic of settings."

Is it any better than what John Huss said, as an old peasant came up and threw another stick on the pyre where Huss was burned to death for heresy? Huss exclaimed, *"O sancta simplicitas!"*

But the question is—was Holmes's admiration for what Jesus said more than a matter of dramatic appreciation?

Maybe. But this again leads to another question, which is—is dramatic admiration any the less authentic, genuine, or true for being dramatic? My faith, the movement of my spirit, and the exaltation of my emotions are no less for being literary or theatrical. I have as much right to cry or laugh over a book or at the theater as I have anywhere else.

❀ 40 ❀

"Eloi, Eloi, lama sabachthani?"

THOSE FEW who remembered and repeated what Jesus said did very well by us, but they did best when they insisted on remembering his cry on the cross, "My God, my God, why hast thou forsaken me?" They who thought he was the Messiah remembered and insisted on recording that he had said this. This, though it contradicted all their hopes, all that he had revealed and they believed. His last words destroyed all he meant to them, all he had left them to hope for and live for. So far as they could see, Jesus had recanted. Yet they preserved his recantation as preciously and scrupulously as they did his teachings and his revelations. Socrates had his Plato. It is fortunate that Jesus did not. For I'd not trust a Plato to record the cry on the cross.

You may be content with the fact that this, the cry on the cross, is a quotation from the Twenty-second Psalm. For a man may express his deepest feelings by a quotation as well as in his own words. Or you may take it as incontestable proof that Jesus was human as well as divine. Or that he did not become wholly divine until he died. Or you may offer it in evidence, as I think Schweitzer does, that Jesus believed until the very end that he was to be the Messiah who would bring the Kingdom in his lifetime. Or you may regard it as the first utterance of modern man, the romantic hero instead of the classical hero, as Holmes once suggested.

Speculation aside, there is a wholly human aspect of triumph in defeat. I know no other better statement of the possibility than William Vaughan Moody's in *The Fire Bringer*.

It is Pandora's song in the first act:

> *"Of wounds and sore defeat*
> *I made my battle stay;*
> *Winged sandals for my feet*
> *I wove of my delay;*
> *Of weariness and fear,*
> *I made my shouting spear;*
> *Of loss, and doubt, and dread,*
> *And swift oncoming doom*
> *I made a helmet for my head*
> *And a floating plume.*
> *From the shutting mist of death,*
> *From the failure of the breath,*
> *I made a battle-horn to blow*
> *Across the vales of overthrow."*

❊ 41 ❊

"Look sharply after your thoughts. They come un-looked for, like a new bird seen on your trees, and, if you turn to your usual task, disappear; and you shall never find that perception again; never, I say—but perhaps years, ages, and I know not what events and worlds may lie between you and its return!"

W<small>HAT WE SHOULD</small> like to know, and never can know, is whether our memory is at all selective. Are we more likely to remember thoughts that turn out on reflection to be usable than those that are not? Is our memory, in other words, either intelligent or appreciative? We shall never know, any more than we can ever know the efficacy of votive offerings in time of danger, because neither the ideas that are forgotten nor the vows that failed are recorded.

It is hard to recapture a sudden thought, one that pops up unexpectedly, for it is usually uncon-nected with the course of our thinking. We do best to go back to where we were standing or to the page we were reading. Better yet, "When found, make a note of."

It is a troublesome and annoying thing, this promiscuous egalitarian attitude that our memory takes toward our wits. It bothered Montaigne as it did Emerson. "But my wits displease me. They usually produce their most profound thoughts, the wildest and those I like the best, unexpectedly and when I am least looking for them. Then they vanish suddenly, if I don't at once secure them. On horseback; at the table; in bed. But mostly on horseback, where my wits are most at large. . . . It happens likewise with my dreams. I recommend my dreams to my memory, for I am likely to dream that I am dreaming, but in the morning, though I can recall their color, gay, or sad, or strange, what else they were, the more I pant after them, the more I drive them into oblivion. So too with the chance thoughts that fall fortuitously into my fancies. All that remains in my memory is their empty reflections, only enough to make me bite my nails in an annoyed pursuit of them, and in vain."

❊ 42 ❊

> "Ne suis-je badault de Paris,
>   De Paris, dis-je, auprès Pontoise?
>   Et d'une chorde d'une toise
>   Sçaura mon coul que mon cul poise."

VILLON WROTE this when he was condemned to be hanged, but the way I have given it is the way Rabelais remembered it when he quoted it, I like to think from memory, near the end of the last chapter of Book Four.

It is possible that Rabelais knew Villon. His sentence was commuted to banishment, and no more is known about him after that, which was in 1463. But Rabelais is telling an anecdote about him as happening in Saint Maixent in Poitou in Villon's old age, and Rabelais may well have been born, according to one account, in 1483. They could have met when Rabelais was very young. I reluctantly think they did not. I share George Saintsbury's hope that they did.

However, here in this quatrain they collaborated. Motteux translated it this way:

"A *silly cockney am I not*
As ever did from Paris come?
And with a rope and sliding knot
My neck shall know what weighs my bum."

And here, without the rhymes I could not find,
is mine:

"*I'm a bum from New York,*
A town near the Bronx.
From a fathom of rope,
My neck will soon learn
The weight of my arse."

Pascal was concerned, and, I think, annoyed at
Montaigne's "nonchalance about salvation, without fear and without regrets." I cannot help quoting
what was once my favorite book, Henry Kingsley's
Ravenshoe: "Charles was to know that a man may
look on death as a going to bed."

❋ 43 ❋

*"I learned today that my ornithology had done me
no service. The birds I heard, which fortunately did
not come within the scope of my science, sang as
freshly as if it had been the first morning of creation . . ."*

TIME WAS BLOWING in Thoreau's face that morning, the fourth of March, 1840, in Concord.

In November 1823, Chancellor von Müller was
visiting in Weimar and on the fourth of November
Goethe took him to Madame Szymanowska's concert, and they had supper afterwards with the Eg-
gloffsteins. There were toasts, and some of them
were to Memory. Goethe interrupted, "I won't admit memory in your sense. That is only a clumsy
way of putting it. Whatever we come on that is
great, beautiful, significant, is not remembered
again from the outside, hunted down, as it were.
Rather it must first be spun from inside of us, be
a part of us, a new and better I begot within us,
and so continually taking form within us, and living and working in us. There is no Past for us to
yearn for. There is only an always Now that forms

itself out of the amplifying elements of the Past. The true yearning for the Past must be productive, and keep creating something better."

And Goethe added, with some feeling, "Have we not all of us felt this in these times? Are we not all of us refreshed, improved, amplified by this kindly and noble vision, which now seems to be forsaking us? No, it cannot be escaping us. It has gone over into our innermost being. It lives in us and with us. Try as it may to escape me, I hold it fast and forever within me."

Henry Ford took the same attitude toward history that Goethe had toward memory. Roger Burlingame writes:

" 'I don't know anything about history,' Henry Ford once said to an interviewer, 'and I wouldn't give a nickel for all the history in the world. The only history that is worth while is the history we make day by day . . .

" 'History is more or less bunk. It is tradition. We want to live in the present, and the only history that is worth a tinker's dam is the history we make today.'

"Ford could never have explained why he had said or thought what he had. Perhaps the word *history* had thrown him back to the Springwells schoolhouse, which had held him in hours when he itched to tinker with an engine. More likely it had suggested the thing that most nearly drove him berserk and resulted in the firing of dozens of his employees—the citing of precedent as proof that

74

something could not be done. The hot rebellion in his quoted speech about 'tradition' hints that he confused history with the inflexible obsessions of method that distinguish the plodder from the creator. (You can't do that! Why? Because it has never been done.) History, in short, delineates the possible, defines the impossible. Have all revolutionaries, perhaps, believed in their hearts that history was bunk?"

Maitland, the great legal historian, went so far as to say that the purpose of history was "explaining, and therefore lightening, the pressure that the past must exercise upon the present, and the present upon the future." Maitland was too much of a lawyer not to pay his respects to the past, and too good a historian to stand in awe of it. Likewise but conversely, Holmes was too much of a historian not to recognize that "historic continuity with the past is a necessity," and too good a lawyer to call it a duty.

Ford did better than either Maitland or Holmes, because he felt no pressure, and saw no necessity. He saw only one aspect of the truth of the matter which Maitland and Holmes were trying to see the whole of, only the aspect that was relevant to his purpose. He carved off his half-truth from the whole truth, which, as Whitehead remarked, "raises the mischief."

Ford lost his temper with history. Goethe burst out at the Egglofsteins when his friends became sentimental over Memory. Both were bent on rid-

ding themselves of all of the Past that did not belong to them, all they had not made their own.

❊ 44 ❊

"PISTOL: No; for my manly heart doth yearn.
Bardolph, be blithe: Nym, rouse thy vaunting
veins: Boy, bristle thy courage up; for Falstaff he
is dead, and we must yearn therefore.

BARDOLPH: Would I were with him, wheresome'er
he is, either in heaven or in hell!

HOSTESS: Nay, sure, he's not in hell: he's in Arthur's
bosom, if ever man went to Arthur's bosom. A'
made a finer end and went away an it had been
any christom child; a' parted even just between
twelve and one, even at the turning o' the tide:
for after I saw him fumble with the sheets, and
play with flowers, and smile upon his fingers'
ends, I knew there was but one way; for his nose
was as sharp as a pen, and a' babbled of green
fields. 'How now, Sir John!' quoth I: 'what, man!
be o' good cheer.' So a' cried out 'God, God,
God!' three or four times. Now I, to comfort him,
bid him a' should not think of God; I hoped there
was no need to trouble himself with any such
thoughts yet. So a' bade me lay more clothes on
his feet: I put my hand into the bed and felt

76

them, and they were as cold as any stone; then I felt to his knees, and they were as cold as any stone, and so upward and upward, and all was as cold as any stone.

NYM: They say he cried out of sack.

HOSTESS: Ay, that a' did.

BARDOLPH: And of women.

HOSTESS: Nay, that a' did not.

BOY: Yes, that a' did; and said they were devils incarnate.

HOSTESS: A' could never abide carnation; 'twas a colour he never liked.

BOY: A' said once, the devil would have him about women.

HOSTESS: A' did in some sort, indeed, handle women; but then he was rheumatic, and talked of the whore of Babylon.

BOY: Do you not remember, a' saw a flea stick upon Bardolph's nose, and a' said it was a black soul burning in hellfire?"

LESLIE HOTSON insists that the Folio reading is right and that Falstaff didn't "babble of green fields" at all, but spoke of "a table of green fields." By this, Hotson assures us, Falstaff was referring to a picture of Sir Richard Grenville, the hero of the Revenge at Flores in the Azores, one against fifty-three. "Table" meant picture in Elizabethan times; and Sir Richard often spelled his name "Greenfields."

It may very well be so, but let us be precise. Hotson is making sense out of a phrase in the Folio in which Shakespear's plays were published after his death. What he claims is that this is the phrase Shakespear wrote in the script and Burbage spoke on the stage.

I am content with the fact that Mistress Quickly told Lewis Theobald later, some time in 1733, that Sir John had babbled of green fields, as he lay dying and she was taking care of him. She told Theobald that she heard him say this and Theobald believed her. He told me, and I believe him. All that Hotson can say against this is that what was printed in the Folio makes better sense than any of us thought it did.

❊ 45 ❊

"Mankind, over the course of the centuries, ought to be considered as a single man who is continually learning. Thus we see how unjust is our respect for antiquity and its philosophers. For, as old age is farthest from infancy, who will not see that the old age of this universal man should not be sought in the age near his birth, but in the time farthest from it? Those we call the ancients are really newcomers and truly in the infancy of mankind. We have added the experience of ages to their knowledge. It is in us that we find the antiquity we revere in them."

WE HAVE two very different attitudes toward the past, and they are reflected in our language. Otherwise I do not think we should be aware of them.

When we think of time simply as the lapse of centuries, years, months, weeks, or even of hours, we face the past.

Things in the past happened *before* our time, and what may come in the future will come *afterwards* and *hereafter*, coming up behind us.

"Prithee, Cynthia, look behind you.
Age and wrinkles will o'ertake you."

We are on a ship headed, *fore* and *aft*, into the past. We speak of a *precedent*, which *precedes* the instant case, and of *previous* and *prior* occasions. If they lie in the future, they follow us *subsequently*. Our *posterity* will come behind us. Our *ancestors* are those who have gone before us. An*tiquity* is an antecedent.

There is nothing new about this. The Greeks, who had everything except a sense of history, had the same attitude toward the past, from the earliest times we know enough about to tell about. You know those lines in Homer where the old men are sitting on the wall, watching Helen walk by and saying, "It was not fate that the Trojans and the well-greaved Greeks suffered so much and so long for such a woman. She looks terribly like a goddess. Even so, and such as she is, let her go home and not be such a nuisance to us and to our children *hereafter*."

The word for *hereafter* is *opisso*, which means *backwards* when it is used of place, and *hereafter* of time. As Liddell and Scott say, "Since the future is unseen and was therefore regarded as *behind* us, whereas *the past* is known and therefore *before* our eyes . . . so also, where *opisso* and *prosso* are opposed, *prosso* must be the past, that which one can see *before* one, and *opisso* the future."

It is quite otherwise when we are thinking of tak-

80

ing future matters into our own hands. Then we *look forward* into the future, and regard the past in *retrospect*. We *foresee* things as best we can, exercising *foresight* and we speak of *hindsight*. We try to *forecast* the future, even *predict* what will happen. We speak of *providence*, and of her sister, *prudence*.

This is all as it should be. When we are not thinking of the future, we turn our backs on it and contemplate the past. When we propose to do something about our future, we turn around and face it.

There is one thing about our contemplation of the past that I do not understand. We don't want to get as close to the past as we can. Visit the American Wing. If the floors are new, and unless the wallpaper has faded, you might almost be walking into the original room, just back from your honeymoon or home from your work. Walk around the fortifications of Carcassonne in the evening, thanks to Viollet Le Duc it will look to you almost as it did to Saint Louis in the thirteenth century. For although you may read, at least you can in my encyclopedia, that Carcassonne "is excellently preserved but very badly restored," it will look more nearly as it did to Saint Louis than your imagination alone could make it seem.

But you don't want to get as close to the thirteenth century as you can. You'd rather have Saint Louis less the ravages of time than Viollet Le Duc less his mistakes. The fact is, what you really want are the ravages of time, and Saint Louis is only a peg to hang them on. You resent the restoration just because it deprives you of the rapture of those ravages. You are a devout antiquarian.

Walter Fisher tells me that touching the same handle, sitting in the same chair, standing on the same spot is different. I stepped carefully about the Great Hall in the castle of Chinon, because half the floor was gone, but I wanted to stand as nearly as possible on the same spot where the Dauphin stood, mingling with the courtiers, to see if Jeanne would pick him out, as, of course, she did. She dropped a curtsy, and said, "My gentle Dauphin, my name is Jehanne la Pucelle. The King of Heaven sends me to you with the message that you shall be anointed and crowned in the city of Rheims, and that you shall be the lieutenant of the King of Heaven, who is the King of France."

Is there any other significant distinction in what I suppose I have to call historicity? Is there any other difference between, let us say, a completely successful fake and the original? Van Meegeren painted pictures so nearly like Vermeer's that they puzzled the experts. Indeed, I am told that litigation over the authenticity of some of the Meegeren-or-Vermeers is still before the courts. If they are Meegeren's, they are all but indistinguishable.

What other significant difference is there between the *Dichtung* and the *Wahrheit* in Goethe's autobiography? Or the history and the fiction in historical novels and fictional biographies? Is there any other peculiar virtue in what did happen over what might have happened? No, but we can't have either without the other.

❊ 46 ❊

"There is nothing like a paradox to take the scum off your mind."

REMEMBER THIS the next time you say something foolish. Holmes had been out to dinner the night before he wrote this to Laski. "The devil," he went on, "set my tongue loose. I told her that I loathed most of the things in favor of which I decided and that you couldn't have a people like the Greeks (temp. Pericles) except on a basis of some kind of slavery."

Now, the fact is, this isn't all foolish. Holmes's conscience required him to make many decisions against his own personal judgment, for he was a conscientious judge. The lady he was talking to was from the South, and Holmes was as gallant as he was conscientious.

But there it is. When you or I say something foolish, we are not just blowing off steam. We are blowing some of the scum off our minds. We are blowing it far enough to one side for at least a glimpse down into the pond of our opinions.

The O.E.D. tells me first that a paradox is "a statement or tenet contrary to received opinion or belief." But this is much less than a paradox has the right to be. You can get more than a glimpse, indeed a vista may be opened, by a true paradox, and the next definition is better: "a statement or proposition which on the face of it seems self-contradictory, absurd, or at variance with common sense, though on investigation or when explained, it may prove to be well founded (or, according to some, though it is essentially true)." What English!

However, take two examples:

"In Thy service is perfect freedom." I used to think that this was a paradox. Now I don't think it is, unless you take "perfect" to mean "complete." Then it is simply self-contradictory. But there is no such thing as a state of complete freedom. You can't be completely free. Even if you want to suppose such a state, in which you are subject to no conditions and no limitations—which would be nonsense, you must want to enjoy your freedom, use it to serve some purpose, some end. "Perfect" here means no more than "best," and what I used to think was a paradox I was not enough of a mystic to understand, is really a simple statement of the belief that the best use you can make of such freedom as you have is to serve God. This is clear enough, and leaves open only the question what you mean by God.

84

George Homans, I think, put it better than the Prayer Book. "Liberty is a beloved discipline."

Another example that used to bother me is Tertullian's remark. "I believe it, because it is absurd." I don't know what it was he found so easy to believe, but his remark is a paradox only if his belief was rational. If it was not rational, he spoke simply and truly. The two kinds of belief come out in Oscar Wilde's "Man can believe the impossible, but man can never believe the improbable." Tertullian was giving an example of Emerson's statement that "a man bears beliefs as a tree bears apples." A good apple tree cannot help bearing apples, and the best believers are those who can't help believing their own beliefs.

However, there are some paradoxes I have too much respect for, like the Beatitudes, to try to resolve, and there are others I can't, though I try as hard as I can. One is the remark Justice Holmes often made: "It is only by effort that a man achieves the inevitable." Or, as it appears in his *Collected Legal Papers*, "The mode in which the inevitable comes to pass is through effort."

I have always admired this gnomic saying as a splendid wisecrack, and I have no doubt Holmes so regarded it. But not long ago I found the most sophisticated of peoples taking this paradox as a matter of course and as trite as it was true.

It was in Homer—near the beginning of the Fifth Book of the *Odyssey*. Odysseus is on the island of Ogygia living with Calypso, a lovely immortal. She wants to keep him and make him immortal too. But he is homesick and he wants to go home to Penelope and Ithaca. Athena appeals to Zeus, and this is what Zeus tells Hermes when he sends him to tell Calypso that she must let Odysseus go:

"Tell this nymph it is our firm decision that Odysseus is to go home, *without the help of god or man*, on a raft, reaching on the twentieth day the land of the Phaeacians, who will send him home on one of their ships, with gifts of bronze and gold and fine clothes. *For it is fated that he shall see his friends and come home to his fatherland.*"

Odysseus is *fated* to reach home. The word is *Moira*, which is Fate, and Fate rules the Olympians as well as mankind. Zeus is saying that it is his wish and that it is also the allotted fate of Odysseus that he shall reach home, but without help from anyone, either god or man. Only his own efforts made it inevitable. This was what Hermes was to tell Calypso, but Homer makes it clear that Odysseus was not told that it was his fate to reach Ithaca, and he was greatly disturbed by the prospect of such a long voyage on a raft. He had good reason to be disturbed. His raft was wrecked, and then he exclaims that his *fate* is death. The word is the same.

Turn it any way you like, and it comes to the same thing. Odysseus is going to get home. It is the decree of fate. But it is going to happen only by his own efforts.

I don't see how to resolve the paradox. It would be flat to say that it was equally inevitable that

86

❈ 49 ❈

"I don't admire the excess of a virtue, such as valor, unless at the same time I see an excess of the corresponding virtue; as in Epaminondas, who combined extreme valor with an extreme gentleness (benignité). For otherwise there is not a rise, but a fall. A man does not show his greatness (grandeur) by going to one extreme, but by reaching both extremes at once, and by filling up all between."

THIS IS Pascal, but I suspect that Montaigne stands behind him. For Montaigne admired Epaminondas enormously, regarding him as one of the three greatest of men—with Homer and Alexander—and the best of the three. And he said that Epaminondas "married the harshest and most violent actions a man can take to a goodness (*bonté*) and a kindness (*humanité*) indeed as delicate (*délicate*) as taught by any philosophy. His courage, so rough, so proud, and so obstinate against pain, against death, poverty, was it nature or was it art that made him tender to an extreme of sweetness (*douceur*) and gentleness (*debonnaireté*) of disposition?"

❋ 50 ❋

"The gentlest thief that ever was."

Yes; and Robin Hood was no whit the less successful. Nay, the stronger and the better, for being gentle.

"You all know something about rats, and in most biological laboratories there are large colonies of them. The rats are used for all kinds of purposes. It is very well known to anybody who has a rat colony that if he doesn't keep the cages clean, and if he doesn't feed his animals well and doesn't take good care of them, they will really be 'rats.' They become very wild, uncontrollable creatures. It is common for mothers to eat their litters, and if you wanted to handle such a rat, you would take a good thick leather gauntlet, so that the rat would not bite you. Now that is so well known that nobody in the laboratory, if he can help it, treats his rats other than with care. He keeps them very clean and he feeds them as well as he knows how. He takes care of them as well as he knows how to. The result is that a laboratory rat is quite a mild creature, quite different from the proverbial rat. If a rat has been treated properly there is no great need to use a leather gauntlet. You can take a rat right out in your hand and he is quite a gentle creature.

"So much for those rather obvious ways of taking care of rats. This information doesn't come from any theoretical or speculative kinds of biology. I have found a very good description in a little manual put out by the Wistar Institute some time ago, describing the care of rats. This manual is actually meant for rat keepers; and it tells you how to go about taking care of rats so that you have a colony that can be used for experimental purposes.

"Their point is that even after you have taken the kind of care that I have just described, you have got to go way beyond that. They say that individual attention shown by handling and petting is essential for the best growth of rats and for securing uniform reactions from them when used as research animals. The rats should have ample opportunity to know their caretakers, and so on; they describe all this gentling treatment to which a rat must be exposed if he really is going to be as useful as possible just as an experimental animal. They finally actually use the word 'gentled.' They refer to such rats as being well-nourished and also as being 'gentled.'

"In the laboratory, we try to get some simple criteria of what that means, and these people give you one very simple one. It is very impressive. When a physiologist has a rat colony, he uses these rats for experiments. One experiment that some physiologists used their rats for was to take out the parathyroid gland. They found that if they took out this gland from rats that had been well nourished but not gentled, eighty-five per cent of those rats died, due to the operation, but that seventy-five per cent of the gentled rats survived. In other words, those rats that had been treated in what you might call a civilized way actually were far more vigorous animals while at the same time far gentler."

❋ 51 ❋

"Thou art a blessed fellow, to think as every man thinks. Never a man's thought in the world keeps the roadway better than thine."

H ARRY, PRINCE OF WALES, and soon to become Henry the Fifth, is speaking to Ned Poynes, his gentleman-in-waiting and his constant companion when the Prince was associating with Falstaff and his Ephesians. Ned is an impecunious younger son, rather a sport and something of a court tennis player. At any rate, he has two pair of silk stockings, one of them peach colored, and only two shirts.

The Prince has just returned to London, tired

with travel and sad on account of the illness of his father, Henry the Fourth. He is joking with Poynes about how much he wants a glass of beer, and about Poynes's two pairs of stockings and two shirts, and how long it is since he's played tennis. Poynes chides him for talking so idly when his father is lying so sick.

The Prince says, "Why, I tell thee, it is not meet that I should be sad now my father is sick, albeit I could tell to thee, as to one it pleases me, for fault of a better, to call my friend, I could be sad, and sad indeed too."

"Very hardly," Poynes replies, "upon such a subject."

"But I tell thee, my heart bleeds inwardly that my father is so sick; and keeping such vile company as thou art hath in reason taken from me all ostentation of sorrow. What would'st thou think of me, if I should weep?"

"I would think thee a most princely hypocrite."

"It would be every man's thought, and thou art a blessed fellow, to think as every man thinks. Never a man's thought in the world keeps the roadway better than thine."

We take a much too superior attitude toward mediocrity, a snobbish attitude. We should do well to appreciate its value, as Harry did in Poynes. Only when it is deliberate, then we do appreciate it. We admire it, and we call it prudence. Then we recognize that mediocrity may very well be a deliberately worldly wisdom.

But a better case has been made for prudence than either deliberate mediocrity or even a worldly and practical wisdom. Socrates, in the dialogue called the "Charmides," as Plato reports it, said that prudence, of all the sciences, was the science of itself as well as of other sciences; and, Socrates added, it is also the science of the lack of science.

This is not so cryptic as it looks. Socrates explained. Only the prudent person really knows himself. He is able to discern what he knows and what he does not know. He has the power of judging what other people know, when indeed they do know, and what they think they know, when they think they know without knowing it.

❋ 52 ❋

"Plutarch says somewhere that he does not find so much difference between one beast and another as he does between one man and another. He is speaking of mental sufficiencies and personal qualities. Truly I find Epaminondas, as I suppose he was, so far from some I know, I mean those capable of common sense, that I'd go farther than Plutarch. I'd say that there is more difference between one man and another than there is between a man and a beast."

THIS IS obviously Montaigne, and I think it is the highest compliment mankind can take with any composure. For the more difference there is between the worst and the best, the better the best must be. I don't know that I have a good reason for this conviction, but this is it.

I was brought up to call it the onion curve. Usually you see only half of it laid on its side, like this:

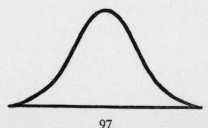

It is the distribution curve. You can see how it looks like an onion if it is stood up and both sides given:

However, the point is the remarkable way that "if we measure and classify a number of persons by any physical characteristic (stature, weight) we find that the results always fall under a curve of probable error. That they should do so is, in fact, a truism. If a number of persons with different degrees of power and resistance are acted on by the same influences, it is most probable that the greatest number of them will reach the same and a mean degree of self-realization, and others in proportion to their power and resistance. The fact has been statistically verified so often, and for such a great variety of physical traits, that we may infer its truth for all traits of mind and character for which we have no units, and which we cannot therefore measure or statistically classify."

Now, to prove my point. Blow up the hump—
or expand the waist of the onion—that is, increase
mediocrity. You pull the points nearer together.
Contrariwise, the fewer average people there are
round the middle, the farther apart are the ends;
the farther Epaminondas is from some of those
Montaigne knew and had in mind; and the more
superlatively sufficient those on top, and the more
superlatively deficient those at the nether end.

❊ 53 ❊

*"Behold, I send you forth as sheep in the midst of
wolves. Be ye therefore wise as serpents and harmless as doves."*

THIS IS the King James version of one of Jesus'
instructions to the twelve apostles, the 16th
verse of the 10th chapter of Matthew, and it strikes
me as a very bad translation of a piece of excellent
advice.

To begin with the word "wise." In the Greek it
is *phronimos*, which means "practically wise,"
"worldly wise." Indeed, "prudent" would be as
good a translation as another. Two other passages
in Matthew, where the same word, *phronimos*, is

used, make this pretty clear. One is the praise for the five "wise" virgins who took care to have oil in their lamps. The other is the "wise" man who built his house on a rock.

But the pernicious mistranslation is the word "harmless," for the Greek *akeraioi* doesn't mean "harmless" at all, nor even "innocent," except in a special sense. Etymologically, *akeraioi* means "unmixed." Actually it means sound and whole. The apostles were to act like men of integrity, not like innocents or simpletons. If I were asked to bet, I'd bet that the translators got the word confused with another Greek word, in which the e was long and not short, *a k é r i o i*, which does mean "harmless."

But, you say, the apostles are to act like doves. We have sentimentalized the dove. There is no reason to think Jesus did. When he was baptized by John, the heavens opened and he saw the Spirit of God descending like a dove and lighting upon him. I decline to sentimentalize the Spirit of God. The apostles were to be as prudent and worldly wise as Mr. Worldly Wiseman himself, and at the same time men of integrity in their faith and calling.

William H. Herndon, Lincoln's law partner, knew him as well as any man. Jack L. Cross picked out some of the things Herndon said about Lincoln and published them in the *Christian Science Monitor* for February 8, 1956. Read this one:

"I do not think that Mr. Lincoln was a hypocrite and yet I know he scarcely trusted any man with

100

his more profound secrets. I had to read them in his facts, acts, hints, face, *as well as what he did not do or say,* however absurd this last expression may appear to be. Mr. Lincoln was a secretive man, had great ambition, profound policies, deep prudences, etc., was retired, contemplative, abstract, as well as *abstracted.* Lincoln was about as shrewd a man as this world ever had and yet he was honest, fair, and manly, incapable of falsehood, of base deception, or of fraud."

❀ 54 ❀

"Sometimes it takes no less skill to know how to profit by good advice than it does to advise yourself."

I SUSPECT that La Rochefoucauld was deliberately understating the difficulty. "No less?" A great deal more! So much more that I sometimes wonder if it is possible to give advice that is worth taking. Of course it helps to ask advice, for then you have to explain your situation. This clarifies the question in your own mind; and it will be a further help if the man or woman whose advice you seek asks you questions.

But when they come to advise you—unless they speak with such authority that it amounts to a command, or unless they only encourage you to do what you wanted to do anyway, and so it isn't advice at all—then I'm not sure what it is.

When the conversation or the consultation comes to the point, and advice is about to be offered, does it not always have to take the form of "If I were you . . ." or "In your place, I . . ."?

But your adviser is not you, and cannot be you, however well he knows you. If he goes on to give you any advice, he must know he will be proceeding on a false premise. Nor is your adviser in your situation. For him it is a moot case, a vicarious problem. There is no reality, no actuality about it. If he goes on to advise you, what Freud called his pleasure-ego will take over from his reality-ego. The best he can do will be to dramatize your situation, and try to play the lead himself.

But you are in the same box. You too are supposing a false premise. You chose him to go to for advice and not someone else, because you were asking yourself, "If I were he, what would I do?" No one but you can answer this question, and you have already made a bad start with this false premise. For you are no more he than he is you.

The fact is both of you are chasing each other round the circumference of a circle, and the problem is in the center. If you and your adviser are much the same sort of person, with similar backgrounds and upbringing, more or less alike in your attitudes toward life and duty and so forth, this is not apparent. But the more different you are, then the more obvious this becomes. You may even find yourselves on diametrically opposite sides of the circumference. You may very well find that it would be appropriate, and accurate, and rude in reply to your adviser's friendly warning, "I'd not do it, if I were you," for you to say, "I'd not do it, if I were you."

The classical example is the story of Alexander and his chief of staff, Parmenion. Darius offered ten thousand talents to ransom his family, whom Alexander had captured, and then as terms of peace, the hand of his daughter and the cession of all Persia west of the Euphrates. Alexander laid these offers before his generals. Parmenion said that were he Alexander he would accept. Alexander replied that he too would accept, were he Parmenion.

If I were to advise the adviser, I'd tell him he'd better confine his advice to some general rule or principle that strikes him as applicable (though he knows that general rules never decide particular cases), to an account of some more or less similar experience of his own (though he knows that precedents never square with instant cases), and to sympathetic attention (which he may well surmise is all you want anyhow).

❊ 55 ❊

SARTRE TELLS about one of his students who came
to him for advice. This student's father had
quarreled with his mother and had been collaborat-
ing with the Nazis. His older brother had been
killed by the Nazis in the invasion of 1940. The
young man wanted to avenge him. He was living
with his mother under this double affliction, the
treason of his father and the death of his brother,
when he was asked to go to England and join the
forces of Free France. This gave him a chance to
avenge his brother and to atone for his father. And
yet he knew that his mother lived only for him and
would be in despair.

Sartre says he refused to advise the boy, partly
because the boy already knew what he would say,
partly because the boy was free and ought to make
the choice himself. Then Sartre explains. The boy's
choice lay between two very different kinds of conduct. One was concrete, immediate, and concerned a particular individual. The other concerned
the vast group of a nation and was, by so much, the
more vague. The boy was hesitating between two
types of morals, one of individual devotion, the

other large and thereby the more open to question. I have been paraphrasing Sartre; I will now translate.

"What could help him choose? The Christian doctrine? No. The Christian doctrine says, Be charitable, love your neighbor, sacrifice yourself for others, take the steep and narrow path. But which path was the steeper? Whom should he love as his neighbor, his brother or his mother? Which would profit him more, the great vague duty of fighting for a nation or the precise duty of helping a particular person to live? Who could decide *a priori*? No one. No written moral code could say. The ethic of Kant says, Never treat others as means, but as ends. But: if I stay with my mother, though I shall be treating her as an end and not as a means, I risk treating as a means all those who are fighting around me; and conversely, if I join those who are fighting, I shall be treating them as ends and thereby I risk treating my mother as a means."

Sartre goes on, "If these standards are vague, and if they are always too vague for the precise and concrete case, all we can do is trust to our instincts. This is what the young man undertook to do, and in our talk he said to me, 'After all, what counts is sentiment. I must choose what is really urging me. If I feel that I love my mother enough to sacrifice the rest to her, my desire for vengeance, for action, for adventure, I stay with her. If, on the contrary, I feel that my love for my mother is not enough, I shall leave her.'

"But how determine the value of a sentiment? What is it that fixed the value of his sentiment for his mother? Precisely the fact that this young man stayed with his mother. I can say, I love my friend enough to give him a certain sum of money, but I can say it only if I have done it. I can say, I love my mother enough to stay with her, but only if I stay with her. I can determine the value of my affection only if I do something which confirms and defines it. So, when I call on my affection to justify my action, I am drawn into a vicious circle."

❋ 56 ❋

"The tigers of wrath are wiser than the horses of instruction."

THIS IS ONE of William Blake's Proverbs of Hell. Near it is a quatrain in which he repeats the thought:

"The pride of the peacock is the glory of God.
The lust of the goat is the bounty of God.
The wrath of the lion is the wisdom of God.
The nakedness of woman is the work of God."

There are times and occasions when wrath is your shrewdest counselor and will give you the best advice. A man is very lucky if he has someone he can go to and talk over a moral problem. Otherwise he's got to stew it out alone—or trust his immediate judgment. In this case, anger will sometimes be the best solvent. His primary problem may very well be whether to turn himself into a deliberative assembly or to trust his instant angry reaction.

But there is one firm qualification. On no account put any trust in anger against yourself. We are more often angry with ourselves than we think, and we are very likely to be more angry with ourselves than we are with others, because we are ashamed of ourselves as well as angry. And if we see no fault in ourselves, we are likely to be somewhat complacent, which has a way of assuaging our anger against others. With this qualification, the tigers of wrath can be very wise counselors.

I put you the case of laughter. The "sudden glory" as Hobbes called it, of a burst of laughter will pass a better judgment than any prolonged appraisal.

❋ 57 ❋

"Fools and clowns and sots make the fringes of everyone's tapestry of life."

I HAVE LESS to say for sots and clowns, unless I am wrong in thinking that by clowns Emerson meant uncouth boors, than I have for fools.

I am not going so far as to follow Blake, that "the road of excess leads to the palace of wisdom" and that "if a fool would persist in his folly he would become wise." His very statements follow their own advice. Nor do I need to point out the overtone of admiration which you sometimes detect when you are told that fools rush in where angels fear to tread. Nor shall I ask you to contemplate a world inhabited wholly by prudent people, prudent women and prudent men. The praise of folly had better avoid even the appearance of excess. I'll follow Poynes and keep to the roadway.

Freedom of speech is as much a matter of ease of thought and spirit as it is of boldness of utterance. We often do better unbuttoned than girded up, better with our shoes off than when we are booted and spurred. As many true words have been spoken in jollity as in jest. Oppenheimer once told a Congressional Committee, "The gossip of scientists who get together is the life blood of physics, and I think it must be in all other branches of science." I must be free to express not only the thought you hate, but also all the thoughts that strike you as simply silly. Clownishness may be the best way to evacuate your mind.

"No, not at all!" you say; and you try to tell me that what I am praising as folly is really only the marginal utility of good sense. I do not agree. I am not praising a marginal utility, but the utility of the marginal, the virtue in being on the fringes as well as of them. Let me go on.

With your stiff good sense, you are confining free speech to debate, pro and con, sticking to the point and seeking the truth. But truth is only a by-product of the process, valuable enough to pay the overhead perhaps, but not enough to pay the help. The help, that is, you and I, want more than truth, a cold dame. We want ease of spirit too. We want to feel satisfied as well as to think we are right.

When I quoted Oppenheimer on the "gossip" of scientists, as I recalled it, he had said "chatter." I don't think he'd object to my mistake, but now I see why I made it. I had in mind what Learned Hand had said about "monkeying around." It was this:

"James Harvey Robinson used to say that we rose from the ape because like him we kept 'monkeying around,' always meddling with everything about us. True, there is a difference, because, although the ape meddles, he forgets, and we have learned, first to meddle and remember, and then to meddle and record. But without the meddling nothing would have happened of all that glorious array of achievement: battleships, aeroplanes, relativity, the proton, neutron, and electron, T.N.T., poison gas, sulfathiazole, the Fifth Symphony, the *Iliad, The Divine Comedy, Hamlet, Faust,* the *Critique of Pure Reason, Das Kapital,* the Constitution of the United States, the Congress of Industrial Organizations, Huey Long, and the New Deal. All these from just 'monkeying around'!"

What about the monkey who is a minority of one? We usually lock him up, Holmes said, but it is possible that we may be mistaken. "If a man does not keep pace with his companions, perhaps it is because he hears a different drummer." The Thoreaus who owe a duty of civil disobedience are not so much disobeying our law as they are obeying another law that is not ours. And we want to know what it is. We had better let them explain it to us.

Why do we expect, why do we all but require, our judges, when they dissent, to file a dissenting opinion, or even individual opinions? Partly, it is true, for their own conscience sake, but chiefly because we want to know why they may be right.

❋ 58 ❋

*"But with unhurrying chase,
And unperturbéd pace,
Deliberate speed, majestic instancy."*

THERE IS NO good reason to think that the United States Supreme Court was quoting from Francis Thompson's *The Hound of Heaven,* when in May 1955 Chief Justice Warren used the words "deliberate speed" in its opinion on the enforcement of its decrees in desegregation cases. But Thompson clearly anticipated, and very precisely described, how the Court expects us to go about it.

May not the adversary process, in the spirit of advocacy, be the best way for a democratic country to enforce a decision, as well as the best way for a Court to make it? On one side, the fanatic fringe, shouting for an immediate heaven of their own making; on the other side, the lunatic fringe, digging their heels in. And in the middle, an irresolute and dissatisfied majority, their feet apart and their arms akimbo. They are the judges. Irresolute, I say, only because they have not yet made up their minds. Dissatisfied, only because they know that a just and wise decision has not yet been reached.

111

I suggest that things get done gradually only between opposing forces. There is no such thing as self-restraint in a people. What looks like it is indecision.

Freedom of speech, freedom for the thought we hate, yes. But this is not enough. This is only toleration, forbearance, patience. The other half is the readiness, the boldness, and the rudeness to speak up and speak out. When Senator George spoke to the American Society of Newspaper Editors in Washington on April 23, 1955, he said, "There is enough disagreement always to make for the safety and security of this country."

Learned Hand put his finger on the same thing in a different context. Asked about the qualities he thought an Overseer of Harvard University should have, he said, "A truly energetic Overseer could make himself a thorn in the side of the Corporation; and it might not be a bad role for a young, contentious, and insensitive Overseer to assume. After all there is something to be said for a person, indifferent to the natural and proper dislike that he will arouse, who meddles about in matters that he does not understand, but has a duty to acquaint himself with. The extent to which he gains popularity with those who are burdened with responsibility is not inevitably the measure of his usefulness."

It may be that truth is best sought in the market of free speech, but the best decisions are neither bought nor sold. They are the result of disagreement, where the last word is not "I admit you're right," but "I've got to live with the son of a bitch, haven't I?"

And may this be the sign of our success, when, as Benny De Voto so shrewdly said, a man of good will can call a Negro a son of a bitch without feeling guilty?

❋ 59 ❋

"Went yesterday to Cambridge and spent most of the day at Mount Auburn; got my luncheon at Fresh Pond, and went back again to the woods. After much wandering and seeing many things, four snakes gliding up and down a hollow for no purpose that I could see—not to eat, not for love, but only gliding."

Mount Auburn is now a cemetery and Fresh Pond is a reservoir, but this was not so when Emerson spent yesterday there in 1834. He saw "many things." I am grateful that the most important—it was the only one he recorded—was "four snakes gliding—but only gliding."

I am tired of being told how wonderful it is that scientific or mathematical theories and equations so beautiful, only beautiful, often turn out to be useful. As if their beauty had to be justified! I don't resent the fact that they may or do prove useful, for this is not the fault of their creators, who conceived them under the auspices of man's highest motive, disinterested joy. They were "only gliding." What I resent is the innuendo that elegance—grace, if you please—needs any justification in works. Beneficence is as far beside the point as benevolence.

I remember Theodore Lyman coming, as he usually did, to lunch at the Porcellian Club and one day announcing that he had discovered a new series of ultra-violet rays. He was pleased to see that they had been called after him and delighted that some German had spelled his name Limmann. But what gave him, he said, deep satisfaction was his belief that his rays could not by any possibility ever be useful to anybody. I now understand that the Lyman series is one of the bases for Planck's quantum theory, and thence of atomic energy.

It is possible that Lyman was quoting a Cambridge mathematician's praise of a theorem, "The best of it all is that it can never by any possibility be made of the slightest use to anybody for anything." Who this mathematician was, I do not know. Holmes quoted him in an article he wrote for the *Harvard Law Review* in 1899, about law and science, where Holmes called it "one of the glories of man" that "he idles away the only hours that fully account for themselves."

Here, it seems to me, lies the point. Our efforts

in these hours we spend pursuing the apparently useless "fully account for themselves." Here is one of our few remaining absolutes, possibly our only one.

It was not the futility, but the monotony, of Sisyphos' task that made it a punishment to keep rolling the stone up the mountain, only to have it fall down again. If he could have picked different stones, or different mountains, or even different ways of pushing the same stone up the same mountain, he might very well have counted it a reward. Certainly this would have been better than just loafing around Hades.

❊ 60 ❊

"Dear Soul, do not pursue with too much zeal
Immortal Life,
But first exhaust the practical mechanics
Of living."

I'M A BIT proud of this translation. I made it in the taxi which took me from Dr. Ward Evans' house to the University of Chicago, where I was to speak at a Law Review dinner that night. I opened what I had to say with these verses. It was a good opening, not just because of the excellence of my translation, but because of the source of the quotation, by which, you may be sure, I introduced it.

Dr. Evans had taken me to lunch at the University Club, and there we ran into Robert Oppenheimer, who was giving some lectures at Northwestern. I told him what I was going to talk about, the law as a craft, and he addressed me in a tongue I recognized as Greek. I asked him if he'd write it out, and he did, on the back of the lunch order.

It was from Pindar, from the Third Pythian Ode. Pindar—when I got home I bought the Loeb edition—was talking about Aesculapius, and how Zeus had killed him, our first physician, with a thunderbolt, because he was presumptuous enough to try to bring a dead man back to life. Pindar says he had been tempted by a big fee. That is not the point.

What I talked about, after this preface out of Pindar, was an attitude, which from the point of view of anything you are doing is its most important aspect. I spoke of the attitude that treats what you do as an end in itself. It may be, for all you know and for all you care, a means toward something else, perhaps something nobler; but this is not your affair, nor your concern—not now, not while you are engaged in doing it. If you are a lawyer, I can make this immediately clear: You are trying cases, not causes. But I can go beyond the law:

> "A servant with this clause
> Makes drudgery divine;
> Who sweeps a room as for Thy laws
> Makes that and th' action fine."

Better even than this from George Herbert is what Ecclesiasticus said:

"So every carpenter and workmaster that laboreth night and day: and they that cut and grave seals, and are diligent to make great variety, and give themselves to counterfeit imagery, and watch to finish a work:

"The smith also sitting by the anvil, and considering the iron work, the vapor of the fire wasteth his flesh, and he fighteth with the heat of the furnace; the noise of the hammer and the anvil is ever in his ears, and his eyes look still upon the pattern of the thing that he maketh; he setteth his mind to finish his work, and watcheth to polish it perfectly:

"So doth the potter sitting at his work, and turning the wheel about with his feet, who is always carefully set at his work, and maketh all his work by number;

"He fashioneth the clay with his arm, and boweth down his strength before his feet; he applieth himself to lead it over; and he is diligent to make clean the furnace:

"All these trust to their hands: and every one is wise in his work.

"Without these cannot a city be inhabited; and they shall not dwell where they will, nor go up and down:

"They shall not be sought for in public counsel, nor sit high in the congregation: they shall not sit on the judges' seat, nor understand the sentence of judgment; and they shall not be found where parables are spoken;

"But they will maintain the state of the world, and all their desire is in the work of their craft."

And, to crown all, to be the motto and the device of all craftsmen, are Peter Viereck's lines,

> "Art, being Bartender, is never drunk;
>   And magic that believes itself must die."

❋ 61 ❋

"Finis opus coronat."

THIS PHRASE has lingered in many distinguished minds. Learned Hand put it into his opinion in the Alcoa monopoly case. Shakespear liked it enough to use it twice, once in French. Hector tells Ulysses that every stone that falls from the walls of Troy

> ". . . will cost
> A drop of Grecian blood; the end crowns all,
> And that old common arbitrator, Time,
> Will one day end it."

I like Ulysses' reply, "So to him we leave it."

And near the end of the second part of *Henry* VI, as Clifford dies, he says, "*La fin couronne les oeuvres.*"

Authors, or perhaps it is their publishers, sometimes put the word *Finis* on the last page of the book. It is quite unnecessary, for the rest of the page is blank and there are no more pages. I have been told that this word *Finis* here is the first word of our phrase, *"Finis opus coronat,"* and that it was what the copyists in the medieval monasteries used to write when they finally came to the end of the manuscript they'd been copying. But it was their own labor that the end was crowning, not the opus they were copying. For to them it was more a labor of devotion than of understanding. They were quite right. The end did crown their menial labor as copyists, as it crowns all menial labor, as it crowned the labor of Time for Hector. Does not Ulysses' reply show that this is what he was thinking?

I think the end crowns the work only when the work is a toil or a chore. Craftsmanship can be a pure joy, and my father used to tell me that the joy he got out of sport, or hunting, or fishing, lay almost all in the doing. Winning the race or making the kill was only about five per cent of the whole of it. The strike of a salmon, he told me, was almost as much of a delight as the kill. I know we lost many of the best races my brother and I sailed with him. "He who has no joy but in enjoyment, who plays only to take the trick, who hunts only for the kill, he has no business," Montaigne said, "meddling in our school."

❋ 62 ❋

"Take egotism out, and you would castrate the benefactors. Luther, Mirabeau, Napoleon, John Adams,
Andrew Jackson; and our nearer eminent public
servants—Greeley, Theodore Parker, Ward Beecher,
Horace Mann, Garrison would lose their vigour."

WHAT MONSTERS we should all be if we were
either egotistic or altruistic, wholly the one
or the other!

Complete altruism would be an abdication of our
selves. We should become something less than human, a cam in a social machine instead of an organ
in the body of our companions. We'd incapacitate
ourselves from playing our parts, from doing our
jobs. For no one but a person in his own right can
properly play his part, for the only part he can
play is his own. Nor do his job, for then it would
be some one else's job, not his.

The fact is, we can't be wholly altruistic in anything we do. What is it that you do for others? Is it
what you think will be good for them? There is a
smell of domination about that. Is it what you
think they want? This is despotism, unless you hap-

pen to be right. Benevolence is not altruism. And if you will consider a moment, you will find that what you admire and love is not altruism, which you do not like, nor benevolence, which you tolerate, it is unselfishness and kindness. We all know how meanly we have treated the word *charity*.

Complete egotism is equally monstrous. Instead of the tail in the snake's mouth, egotism is the head biting the tail, and soon even the body cannot tell which is which.

The Golden Rule is a precept, but it is also a statement of the right relation between egotism and altruism and a reconciliation of their conflicting claims. I think Luke puts it best: "And as ye would that men should do to you, do ye also to them likewise." The "likewise" is better than Matthews' "even so."

To begin with, the Golden Rule assumes that both of us are free. Then it goes on to allot to each an equivalent, if not an equal, amount of egotism and altruism.

Your altruism is set on a high standard, for it is the standard you expect of others, which, in this world, is so often higher than you too often set for yourself. It is likewise highly egotistic, for plainly you expect similar high conduct from the other fellow. Not that there is any bargain about it, but there are great expectations, and they are all but purposeful. There is enough selfishness to scare the Rotary International into dropping its motto, "He profits most who serves best," which it did at its fortieth annual meeting in 1949. The AP reported that "the Rotary Board of Directors abandoned this motto, because it was felt the word 'profit' might be misconstrued." No, it was too true. The directors kept the other motto of the Rotary, "Service above self," which makes no sense and so could not possibly be misconstrued.

I think it is worth noting that the Golden Rule specifies no particular kind of conduct, nor any end or purpose or desired result. It is not religious, even as a precept. It applies to all kinds of conduct, from the most momentous sacrifices to the social amenities. Lord Chesterfield found it the best rule he knew to assure his son success in society. "Do as you would be done by is the surest method I know of pleasing."

The last word on the Golden Rule so far as I am concerned, goes to George Orwell. He wrote that "the subject of *Lear* is renunciation, and it is only by being wilfully blind that one can fail to understand what Shakespeare is saying," which is this, Orwell went on: "Give away your lands if you want to, but don't expect to gain happiness by doing so. Probably you won't gain happiness. If you live for others, you must live for others, and not as a roundabout way of getting an advantage for yourself."

William Empson, who quotes this, and from whom I got it, adds, "The critic who has most nearly anticipated Orwell seems to be Freud, who said that the meaning of the play was the tragic refusal of the old man to 'renounce love, choose death, and make friends with the necessity of dying.' "

To go back to Emerson's remark about the egotism of the benefactors, Holmes wrote my mother on February 27, 1921, "Abolition of self-love I think undesirable rot. As I often have observed nature makes self-love an instrument of altruism and martyrdom, but the self-love is not required to know it, although it is more intelligent if one does. I refer to the process by which the game, begun as a means, becomes an end in itself and the merchant and lawyer and the rest sacrifice health to the pursuit of their calling."

❊ 63 ❊

"I think nature takes care of our altruism for us, and that a man who thinks he has been an egotist all his life, if he has been a true jobbist (you remember my club?), will find on the Day of Judgment that he has been a better altruist than those who thought more about it."

MANY OF YOU, I am sure, have heard about Holmes's club. It is the Society of Jobbists. Some of you belong, and could tell us more about it than I can. Holmes was its first President, until his death in 1935. Learned Hand succeeded him, and is the President now.

There was a time when Hand used to deny that he was even a member. This was not because it was a secret society. I have known members who were willing to talk fairly freely about it, its aims and some of the qualifications for membership, but not its members. No list of its members has ever been published. Perhaps it is secret, but I am inclined to think that the reason Hand refused to admit he belonged was simply false modesty.

Very little about the Society has ever been published. In a letter to Lady Askwith on March 3, 1915, which you will find in Mark Howe's biography, Holmes wrote, "This society recognizes that altruism and egotism are only the ways you feel about your work in the half hour's recess, or on the usual Saturday half holiday—but that when you are on your job, if you do it well, you are neither altruist nor egotist, and that the important thing is how you do your job and not how you think or feel about it afterwards. Hence members are to be allowed their idiosyncrasy in recess—if they forget it while they are at their task. It is a club for the abolition of altruism as a requirement of salvation." In another of Holmes's letters, to Wu on March 26, 1925, Holmes wrote that the members "were free to be egotists or altruists on the usual Saturday half-holiday provided they were neither while on the job. Their job is their contribution to the general welfare and when a man is on that, he will do it better the less he thinks either of himself or his neighbors, and the more he puts all his energy into the problem he has to solve."

This is brief, but illuminating. I may add that the Saturday half holidays were later extended to the whole day, when the Society went on a five-day week.

Hand, of course, knows more about the Society than anyone except Holmes, and in 1930, on the occasion of the ninetieth anniversary of Holmes's presidency, Hand gave us the fullest account of the Society that we possess.

"Are you a member of the Society of Jobbists, or do you know the guild? If not, let me tell you of it. All may join, though few can qualify. Its president is a certain white-haired gentleman, with a keen blue eye, and a dangerous turn for dialectic. But the other members need not and do not fear him, if they keep the rules, and these are very simple. It is an honest craft, which gives good measure for its wages, and undertakes only those jobs which the members can do in proper workmanlike fashion, which of course means no more than that they must like them. Its work is very various and indeed it could scarcely survive in these days, if the better known unions got wind of it, for quarrels over jurisdiction are odious to it. It demands right quality, better than the market will pass, and perhaps it is not quite as insistent as it should be upon standards of living, measured by radios and motor-cars and steam heat. But the working hours are rigorously controlled, because for

125

five days alone will it labor, and the other two are all the members' own. These belong to them to do with what they will, be it respectable or not; they are nobody's business, not even that of the most prying moralists.

"I confess that I have often applied for admission and have been always rejected, though I still live in hope. The membership is not large, at least in America, for it is not regarded with favor, or even with confidence, by those who live in chronic moral exaltation, whom the ills of this world make ever restive, who must be always fretting for some cure; who cannot while away an hour in aimless talk, or find distraction for the eye, or feel agitation in the presence of fair women. Its members have no program of regeneration; they do not agitate; they decline to worship any Sacred Cows, American or Russian, but none the less, you must be careful how you thwart them. They are capable of mischief; for you must not suppose, because they are amiable and gay and pleasure-loving, because they are not always reverent, that they are not aware of the silences, or that they do not suppose themselves to have embarked upon a serious enterprise when they began to breathe. You may go so far with them in amity and fellowship; you may talk with them till the cocks crow, and differ as you like and as you can, but do not interfere with the job, and do not ask for quarter if you do—you will not get it. For at bottom they have as much faith as you, and more, for it is open-eyed and does not wince. They have looked in most of the accessible closets, and though many are too dark to explore and they know little about what is in them, still they have found a good many skeletons, taken them apart, and put them together. So far as they have got, they are not afraid of them, and they hope that those they have not seen may not be worse than the few they have.

"The Society goes along quite jauntily; the jobs and the two days off are all a good deal like play. When you meet a member, you are aware of a certain serenity that must come from being at home in this great and awful Universe, where man is so little and fate so relentless. *Fais ce que voudra* will do as well for their legend as it did for the Abbey of Thélème. But they study to find out what they really do want; they remember what Goethe said: 'Let the young man take care what he asks in his youth, for in his age he shall have it.' It sounds easier than it really is to join the Society. I fancy one must learn the rules apperceptively, for it is no use trying to get them by rote; I have tried that way and it does not work. You had best go to the President, for while some of the other members no doubt are as adept as he, after all he has grasped the underlying idea so well that if you get his exposition, you need not go further. He knows about it all, and he is very willing to take in neophytes."

You will note that neither the importance, nor even the dignity of the job has anything to do with it. It is not a matter of magnitudes, but of attitudes. I don't know who the man was that Frances Corn-

ford wrote these verses about, but I do know he was
a member, and I'm sure she did.

> "Now when his hour shall strike
> For this old man,
> And he arrives in Heaven late
> He can
> To Peter and the Angel Gabriel,
> Having completely known,
> Completely tell
> What it was like
> To lean upon a gate;
> And knowing one thing well
> He need not fear his fate."

I do not see why he was apprehensive. Perhaps it
was because neither Gabriel nor Peter are members,
and he was not certain they would understand.

❋ 64 ❋

"Bid a singer in a chorus, Know Thyself, and will
he not turn for the knowledge to his fellows in the
chorus and to the tune?"

I PICKED this up in the Loeb edition of Epictetus.
It is a fragment, quoted by Stobaeus in his *Ec-
logues*. So we must take it as it stands, alone and out

of its context. We cannot consult its fellow sentences.

The best reason to want to be free is to be yourself, and the best reason to want to be yourself, as fully and wholly yourself as you can be, is to sing your part in a chorus. For only when we sing our part the best we can, are we most ourselves. Why else do you want freedom anyhow? How else, come down to it, can you have it? Try to make a fire with one log. There are a few, a very few, who can turn it to account by themselves. All the rest of us must recognize that unless we use what freedom we have in the work we do with others, we have none. For when all is said, and so much of it so well said, we are left with the sobering thought that what freedom we don't use simply does not exist. There's no such thing as unused freedom. Freedom is not only perishable. It is a quality of an activity. It's like fresh fruit. Unless you eat it, it's soon garbage.

One of the things a singer in a chorus learns about himself is the pure pleasure of working *with* others, which transcends the pleasure of doing things *for* others. At any rate, it is a purer joy, because what you are doing and even why you are doing it become very nearly irrelevant. Collaboration, co-operation, itself and by itself, ennobles whatever you are doing. The nobility of your purpose, in its own way, will add its virtue to your pleasure, but if you look closely, you will see that it is an addition. It is important. It may be more than important. But it is supplementary. Make the work as trivial or as boring as you wish. There will remain the unalloyed joy of collaboration. Degrade it, defile it with vicious motives or ignoble ends. Only your conscience can take all the joy out of it. Fail. You have lost no more than success; and if the job was difficult, the greater was the joy of undertaking it and trying to do it together with your fellows.

Start with the simply physical. Two men on a cross-cut saw. Two men with sledge hammers pounding on one spike. A working party. A road gang. A gun crew. A football team. A ballet. A theatrical company on the road. Suit yourself.

Step it up into danger. A combat patrol. A bomber crew. I suggest to you that the real plane consists not of the wings and the fuselage and the motors—they are only temporarily indispensable—but in the crew and their intercom system.

Add the intellectual. Two or more can collaborate on a textbook. Many can co-operate on a scientific investigation. It is hard to tell how much of an as-told-to autobiography is vicarious. But very few good novels have been written by collaborators. Too few? Why is it that playwrights seem to be able to collaborate with better success than novelists?

You will add your own examples, and you will come to the prototype of all collaboration, sexual intercourse. There at its peak is the apparent paradox of finding your own best and full satisfaction only in the giving of it. As Montaigne said, other pleasures may be recompensed in different ways, but this one can be repaid only in the same coin; and he added, "Indeed, in this pastime the pleasure I give tickles my imagination more sweetly that what is given me."

There the last and least distinction between two selves is extinguished in a collaboration which transcends both purpose and consequence. There the physical and the emotional are reconciled. Plato, seeking an analogy, compares his dialectic, where question and answer come nearer and nearer to a definition, mind working on mind, to the sexual act. "It was necessary that mind should work on mind, by short question and answer, or an expert employment of the dialectic process, in order to generate new thoughts and powers; a process which Plato, with his exuberant fancy, compares to copulation and pregnancy, representing it as the true way, and the only effectual way, of propagating the philosophic spirit."

We all know that the achievement of anything we are proud of requires a certain lift of the spirit. Let me call it passion. We know the intensity that is drawn tight by a cause, all the way from the cause that is hopeless, which makes it sacred and its service religions, to success, which makes it fun. We know the spur of curiosity or the prospect of profit. We neglect the obvious and commonplace virtue in merely and simply working together with others.

There are greater pleasures and nobler passions than working together. I ask you not to mistake my praise. What I have singled out is only one ingredient in the soul of man, small and simple, and humble enough to be neglected. Yet it is, I believe, one of our few absolutes; and by this I mean that it has no comparable alternative, and that it is its own purpose and its own end. It begets nothing but itself, and most of us need no more, either to do our best or, what is perhaps not so important, to know most about ourselves.

❋ 65 ❋

"He who thought it not good for man to be alone, preserve me from the more prodigious monstrosity of being never by myself!"

THERE IS an episode near the start of the first chapter of *All Quiet on the Western Front,* which a publisher's prudery kept out of the first American translation. The three buddies found that the only place they could enjoy any privacy was in the field latrine, which consisted of a number of small wooden shacks, movable, with handles on the sides. They took three and set them down in a circle. There they would sit, smoking, reading their letters from home, and playing skat on the cover of a margarine tub.

There is a contrariety, even a downright inverse ratio, between privacy and authority. Take any authoritarian regime—our military establishments, our monastic orders, many educational institutions —and you can almost measure the height of authority by the rise of the privy as a social center.

"A free society can exist only when public spirit is balanced by an equal inclination of men to mind their own business. . . . No society is capable of sustaining the unremitting interest of all its citizens all the time, or even of most of its citizens most of the time, in the problems of the larger society. . . .

"Democracy requires the occasional political participation of most of its citizenry some of the time, and a moderate and dim perceptiveness—as if from the corner of the eye—the rest of the time. It could not function if politics and the state of the social order were always on everyone's mind. If most men, most of the time, regarded themselves as their brother-citizens' keepers, freedom which flourishes in the indifference of privacy, would be abolished, and representative institutions would be inundated by the swirl of plebiscitary emotions—by aggressiveness, acclamation and alarm."

A few pages further on, Shils adds,

"In an individualistic society where the sense of institutional identity is often weak and where the principle of publicity is so central to the national culture, the only relationship between publicity and secrecy would, if men were reasonable, be one of conflict.

"The situation is not, however, quite so simple. There are points at which publicity, overreaching itself, also doubles back on itself. At the extremes there is an affinity of opposites. Whereas most Americans take publicity in their stride and are affronted by secrecy, there are some, a small but vigorous minority, who are equally and extremely attracted by both.

"There are persons for whom publicity is not just part of the accepted rules of the game of American social life, but to whom it is a means to salvation itself. Like secrecy, which might be functional or magical, so publicity can be practiced and accepted as the normal pattern of relationships among individuals and institutions or it can be endowed with sacred properties and surrounded with excited sentiments.

"The American love of publicity is of both types. The former predominates, but there is always a tinge of the latter in it, particularly among the professionals of publicity. In a small sector of the population the balance is reversed and the magical protectiveness of publicity has the upper hand. It is in these circles that the preoccupation with secrecy is greatest—secrecy not in any rational sense, but rather secrecy as a source of danger and as a saving refuge. There is an irrational adhesion of the three elements: fear of secrets, dependence on secrets, and dependence on publicity."

❊ 66 ❊

"I like people who can do things. When Edward and I struggled in vain to drag our big calf into the barn, the Irish girl put her finger into the calf's mouth and led her in directly."

THE SAME STRAIN of admiration appears in Emerson's *Essay on Plato* where he says of the Greeks that they "cut the Pentelican marble as if it were snow, and their perfect works in architecture and sculpture seemed things of course, not more difficult than the completion of a new ship at the Medford yards, or new mills at Lowell. These things are in course, may be taken for granted."

Your best, your very best, must be done as a matter of course, as a sequel of yourself. It drops from you as a part of yourself. In the hand of a good surgeon, the knife is another or a longer finger. A golf club or a tennis racket in the hand of a good player is an extension of his arm. A good pilot, they say, flies with his arse.

When Dr. Rabi, now the chairman of the General Advisory Committee of the Atomic Energy Commission, testified for Oppenheimer before the Gray

Board in 1954, and Gray suggested to him that not all the derogatory information available to the Board was available to him, Rabi said, "It may be. On the other hand, I am in possession of a long experience with this man, going back to 1929, which is twenty-five years, and there is a kind of seat-of-the-pants feeling on which I myself lay great weight."

There was the professor at the Harvard Medical School, very possibly Dr. Holmes, who at the end of the term wrote out on the blackboard a list of the points he had been at pains to make throughout the course. As the students copied them out, one student asked if these were the things thay were to be sure not to forget. "No," said the professor. "These are what you must have forgotten if you are to be a good physician."

It is not the subconscious that is doing so well for us. We are not unaware of what we are doing or of how we are doing it. We are wholly aware, completely and perfectly aware. So much so that there is no awareness to spare to watch ourselves doing it. It is the complete collaboration of the I and the Me that William James distinguishes and discusses in that chapter on "The Self" in his *Psychology*. The I is not watching the Me. It is too busy lending a hand. "Kind, ich hab' es klug gemacht," Goethe said, "Ich habe nie über das Denken gedacht." "Boy, I'll say that I've been clever: I think, but think of thinking never."

As George Luks told Harrison Tweed, an artist should always hope there was standing behind him an angel with an ax, knowing that the angel will strike him down just before he "finishes" the picture. For then the I is about to take over, pushing the Me aside, and try to "finish" the picture by itself.

The Japanese have elevated this inquiry into one's self to a discipline and a cult. I do not mean a religious cult, nor a mystic discipline. Do not be put off by any such thought, when you read, as I hope you do, what Ruth Benedict tells us in her book, *The Chrysanthemum and the Sword.*

"A long series of Japanese words name the state of mind the expert in self-discipline is supposed to achieve. Some of these terms are used for actors, some for religious devotees, some for fencers, some for public speakers, some for painters, some for masters of the tea ceremony. They all have the same general meaning, and I shall use only the word *muga,* which is the word used in the flourishing upper-class cult of Zen Buddhism. The discipline of this state of expertness is that it denotes those experiences, whether secular or religious, when 'there is no break, not even the thickness of a hair' between a man's will and his act. A discharge of electricity passes directly from the positive to the negative pole. In people who have not attained expertness, there is, as it were, a non-conducting screen which stands between the will and the act. They call this the 'observing self,' the 'interfering self,' and when this has been removed by special kinds of training the expert loses all sense that 'I am doing

137

it.' The circuit runs free. The act is effortless. It is 'one-pointed.' The deed completely reproduces the picture the actor had drawn of it in his mind.

"Suzuki, the great authority on Zen Buddhism, describes *muga* as 'ecstacy with no sense of *I am doing it*,' 'effortlessness.' The 'observing self' is eliminated; a man 'loses himself,' that is he ceases to be a spectator of his acts. Suzuki says: 'With the awaking of consciousness, the will is split into two . . . actor and observer. Conflict is inevitable, for the actor (self) wants to be free from the limitations of the observer-self. Therefore in Enlightenment the disciple discovers that there is no observer-self, 'no soul entity as an unknown or unknowable quantity.' Nothing remains but the goal and the act that accomplishes it.' "

❀ 67 ❀

"Letting 'I do not' wait upon 'I can.' "

I HAVE BEEN told that Galileo, as soon as he heard that some Dutchman had invented a microscope, at once made a telescope, with which Galileo then observed the satellites of Jupiter.

Gunder Haegg's world record mile in 4 minutes

1.4 seconds, which he made in 1945, stood for nine years. A 4-minute mile seemed impossible, until a British medical student named Roger Bannister ran a mile in 3 minutes 59.4 seconds in a meet at Oxford on May 6, 1954.

Within a couple of months an Australian, John Landy, beat it by almost a second and a half, at 3 minutes 58 seconds. And within two years (June 1956), eight men had beaten 4 minutes fourteen times.

Mount Everest had never been climbed until Edmund Hillary and Tenzing reached the top on May 29, 1953. Within three years, in May 1956, four members of a Swiss expedition climbed to the top, two by two, on successive days, Ernst Schmeid and Jurg Karmet, and then Adolph Reist and Hans von Gunten.

In 1945 a team of scientists under Robert Oppenheimer and Leslie Groves made an atomic bomb at Los Alamos. Four years later the Russians made one. How much longer would it have taken them if they had not known it could be done?

❁ 68 ❁

"Take, therefore, no thought for the morrow: for the morrow shall take thought for the things of itself. Sufficient unto the day is the evil thereof."

THIS IS the last verse in chapter 6 of Matthew. "Take no thought" may be right, but the other meaning of the Greek word, *merimnesate*, is "Do not be anxious," and it fits into the context better.

Jesus is talking about food and drink and clothes. "Is not the life more than meat, and the body more than raiment?" Read the whole chapter, and you will see that Jesus' advice was neither improvident nor impractical. On the contrary. Nor is it simply eschatological, in immediate expectation of the Last Judgment. It was simply good practical advice. Sir William Osler told his students at McGill:

"As to your method of work, I have a single bit of advice, which I give with the earnest conviction of its paramount influence in any success which may have attended my efforts in life—Take no thought for the morrow. Live neither in the past nor in the future, but let each day's work absorb your entire energies, and satisfy your widest ambition."

❋ 69 ❋

*"Beshrew thee, Cousin, which didst lead me forth
Of that sweet way I was in to despair."*

Richard the second. Morbidly romantic?
Yes, but there's a hard core to it, the feeling
of security that comes from the acceptance of the
possibility of the worst that could happen.

❋ 70 ❋

"Give us this day our daily bread."
"Give us day by day our daily bread."

The first is the way it is in Matthew. The word
is *semeron*, which means *today*.

The second is from Luke, where the word is
to kath' emeran, which means *daily*.

"The greatness of Christianity—the greatness of

any valuable religion—consists in its 'interim ethics.' The founders of Christianity and their earlier followers firmly believed that the end of the world was at hand. The result was that with passionate earnestness they gave free rein to their absolute ethical intuitions respecting ideal possibilities without a thought of the preservation of society. The crash of society was certain and imminent. 'Impracticability' was a word which had lost its meaning; or rather, practical good sense dictated concentration on ultimate ideas. The last things had arrived; intermediate stages were of no account."

If the end of your world may come at any time, like a thief in the night, practical good sense dictates very different conduct than it does when you are sure that everything is gradually and inevitably getting more and more comfortable and good, or even going to stay tolerable. In a bombed city only an interim ethics makes sense, apparently to the astonishment, admiration, and frustration of the purely military mind. The curve of morale rises as the bombs fall.

The effect of any common emergency is to put ethics on an interim basis. Either that or ethics are eliminated. If we are all perishing or about to perish, there is no longer time to choose between the better and the worse, between the more or the less practical. It becomes a question of all or nothing.

What puzzles me is that we are now, for the first time, faced with the real possibility that the end of our world may very well be at hand; and yet I see no sign of any interim ethics.

Is this because the end would be our own doing, come by our own explosion of our own bombs? It would seem that man can never stand in awe of himself, and I see no reason why he should.

We are living in what Harlow Shapley has called the Pax Urania, and we are monkeying with our descendants, to what extent nobody knows. Nor toward what result. We seem to be taking it for granted that any mutations will be for the bad, but there is no a priori reason to think that this is so. The only experience we have is not with ourselves, but with plants and insects, fruit flies and flowers. For all we know, many, maybe most, of our self-induced human mutations may be for the better. We may even be generating a race of angels.

Mankind has three powerful weapons: the nuclear bomb, as we all know; martyrdom, as the youth of Hungary are reminding us; and passive resistance, as the Negro bus patrons in Alabama are showing us.

❋ 71 ❋

"I do not fear tomorrow, because I have seen yester-
day and I love today."

THIS I SAW in the window of the Swedenborgian
bookshop on Bowdoin Street, by the State
House, in Boston. It was ascribed to William Allen
White.

❋ 72 ❋

"He builded better than he knew,
The conscious stone to beauty grew."

THE STONE is at first sensitive, but it becomes
sentient, and then conscious, Emerson per-
ceived, as the work progresses. Thus, under the eye
of the architect and the hand of the workman, it
grows to a greater beauty than they knew how to
make.

Montaigne, whom Emerson may here be turning into verse, made this clear. "The work, of its own force and fortune, can second the workman and surpass him, beyond his own invention and knowledge." Work in process, starting from scratch, overtakes and passes the workmen.

Montaigne gives this as the reason why men are no better judges of their own work than others. I suggest that it is also a mark and measure of the best workmen, that they are able to make things that are better and larger than they are. To do this is the highest compliment.

A child is being well educated only when it is being made more and more independent of the parent. A good poem is bigger and better than the poet. The good leader evokes more than he calls for. The good organizer or administrator finds himself at the head of an institution that transcends his achievement. It is the difference between achievement and creation.

✳ 73 ✳

"The mind of Caesar. It is the reverse of most men's. It rejoices in committing itself. To us arrive each day a score of challenges; we must say yes or no to decisions that will set off chains of consequences. Some of us deliberate; some of us refuse the decision, which is itself a decision; some of us leap giddily into the decision, setting our jaws and closing our eyes, which is a sort of decision of despair.

"Caesar embraces decision. It is as though he felt his mind to be operating only when it is interlocking itself with significant consequences."

THIS IS what Sosthenes, Caesar's doctor, says about his patient in Thornton Wilder's *The Ides of March*; and I take it that Wilder is as reliable as Plutarch, or Suetonius, or Shakespear, or Shaw, or any of the others.

Let me say that the question which is the real Caesar is just as idle an inquiry as who is the real Falstaff or the real Mistress Quickly. They are all real, in their own ways.

You remember the way Shakespear put it, "Dan-

146

ger knows full well that Caesar is more dangerous than he."

A general principle is only the avenue up which we approach a decision, just as an abstraction expresses only our attitude toward taking a decision. Its perspective puts the highlight on the point or the facet which reflects our interest or concern. We have to get closer up before we can make a good decision, and it calls for great courage, or a nature like Caesar's, to go up to a problem instead of waiting for it to come to us.

The best advice is A. Lawrence Lowell's. He used to say, and I think he wrote it somewhere, that we should do first the things we can put off doing. As you see, he was a man who accepted responsibility gladly and who made decisions eagerly. The things that you can't put off will speak up for themselves and press themselves upon you. In a sense, they use you to get themselves done, and work themselves out through you.

Lowell told Graham Wallas much the same thing:

"The President of Harvard once described to me a mental expedient not unlike Sir Warren Fisher's. He said that he had tried to train himself to begin the day by doing what *could* be put off and leaving till later what could not be put off. That which 'can be put off' means not only that which will not be mechanically brought forward by an interview already fixed or an urgent letter on the desk; it also often means some question which, without a special effort of volition, we should be inclined to put off, a problem with slightly uncomfortable associations, or an inchoate train of still vague and only partially conscious thought which will drift into forgetfulness unless the 'salt box' is used."

There is much to be said for patience. "How poor we are without patience!" Plan ahead, yes. Ponder the possibilities. It is the better part of courage to be tentative. Do not finally decide until the insistence of events has brought you nose to nose with necessity. This is so, not only for the sake of intervening facts, but on account of the soft and speculative condition of your mind when it is considering only possibilities, before it is confronted with action.

❊ 74 ❊

"Nothing noble is done without risk."

I found this in Gide's *Journal*. It is Montaigne, *"Rien de noble se fait sans hasard."* His spiritual half-cousin, Benjamin Franklin, gave us its complement: "The way to be safe is never to be secure," said Poor Richard.

Hotspur, reading a letter which gives him some prudent advice, " 'The purpose you undertake is dangerous.' Why that's certain. 'Tis dangerous to take a cold, to sleep, to drink; but I tell you, My Lord Fool, Out of this nettle, Danger, we pluck this flower, Safety."

On the other hand, John Paul Jones wrote to a friend, "And I have never ceased to mourn the failure of the Count de Grasse to be as imprudent as I could not have helped being on that grandest of all occasions."

Jones was referring to the way the Count de Grasse broke off his action with the British fleet in the Chesapeake Capes. By withdrawing he was able to cut off Cornwallis, who then had to surrender to Washington at Yorktown.

What selfish folly, had the Count de Grasse put Yorktown at hazard for his own glory!

❀ 75 ❀

"Yet, after all, the truly efficient laborer will not crowd his day with work, but will saunter to his task, surrounded by a wide halo of ease and leisure, and then do what he loves best. He is anxious only about the fruitful kernels of time. . . . Some hours seem not to be occasion for any deed, but for resolves to draw breath in. . . . Our resolution is taking root or hold on the earth then, as seeds first send a shoot downward which is fed by their own albumen, ere they send one upward to the light."

THIS WAS on Sunday in *A Week on the Concord and Merrimac Rivers*. "Saunter to his task" is the phrase that lingers in my mind. Thoreau is talking about the great problem of how a man may best approach a difficult task. He says a man should "saunter" to it. He should be anxious only about the hour and the occasion, whether he'd better draw breath for a while more until resolution takes deeper root. But the approach, and the spirit of the approach, is the important thing.

Lawrence Henderson used to speak of circling down to a problem in a spirally closer approximation. And Henderson added that you were not to ask for too much. "Fix once for all in your mind," he said, "that you are seeking *rough* approximations and *sufficient* probabilities, cheering yourself with the assurance that all the results of all the experimental sciences are but approximations and probabilities." How else determine the relevance or the importance of anything? How otherwise make your mind up about anything?

I think of this approach to a problem in Yeats's phrase in *Sailing to Byzantium*, "perne in a gyre." I still do, although Yeats says that a "perne" is a spool or bobbin. I stick by the O.E.D. that told me that a perne is a buzzard. Not that Yeats meant it my way, but I like it better.

There is another thing about sauntering up to your task. When we were in Kenya, my father, my brother, and I would hunt in the morning, and then in the afternoon one of us would go out to shoot a kongoni, or a wildebeeste, or a zebra, to eat. There was no possibility of stalking on the open plain. The game were grazing in the open, and we'd walk toward them. But we would walk diagonally toward the nearest. If you walked directly toward them, they'd all move off. But if we seemed to be passing the herd, they'd go on grazing. So we'd diagonally saunter; and I remember that my native gunbearer always advised me to think of other things. When we got within a hundred yards or so, I'd drop on one knee and shoot for the shoulder.

So likewise with a difficult problem. We come to

learn that when we formulate and state it, we are already engaged toward an answer. Sometimes, indeed, to state a question is a first step in the process of answering it, and for all you know, it may be a step in a wrong direction, which you learn too late.

So you approach a problem cautiously. If it is possible, you stalk it. If this is not possible, you saunter toward it, circle it a couple of times, approximate it, or, as I did with the kongoni, approach it diagonally, all for fear that your very observing of it will affect it, alter it, and so lead you to misstate it.

The atomic scientists are in the same, if not worse, case. What Bohr and Heisenberg said about the observation of physical objects—they were dealing with atomic physics—is equally easily applicable to mental conceptions, as they very well knew. I give you a summary of their theory in the words of Schrödinger.

"We cannot make any factual statement about a given natural object (or physical system) without 'getting in touch' with it. This 'touch' is a real physical interaction. Even if it consists only in 'looking at the object,' the latter must be hit by light-rays and reflect them into the eye, or into some instrument of observation. This means that the object is *interfered with* by observing it. You cannot obtain any knowledge about an object while leaving it strictly isolated. The theory goes on to assert that this disturbance is neither irrelevant nor completely surveyable. Thus after any number of painstaking observations the object is left in a state of which *some* features (the last observed ones) are known, but *others* (those interfered with by the last observation) are not known, or not accurately known. This state of affairs is offered as the explanation why no complete, gapless description of a physical object is possible."

There is the same interaction between me and a difficult problem as there is between the atomic physicist observing the inside of the atom. If this interaction can neither be controlled, nor avoided, nor even itself be observed, as they say it cannot, then it behooves me to choose my approach to a difficult problem with caution and circumspection. Saunter to your task.

❊ 76 ❊

"In a similar light-hearted way it was pointed out that, as the state of an atomic system requires observation for its definition, so the course of psychological phenomena might be irretrievably altered by the very effort to probe them—as a man's thoughts are altered by the fact that he has formulated and spoken them. It is, of course, not the fact that observation may change the state of an atomic system that gives rise to the need for a complementary description; it is the fact that, if the observation is to be meaningful, it will preclude any analysis or control of that change, that is decisive."

I DON'T KNOW how an atom likes being stared at, nor how it behaves under scrutiny, but I've been told enough not to be light-hearted about any thing about atoms, far less about their analogies in the ordinary affairs of men.

One analogy seems to me lies in the jury. Its deliberations are secret. It is forbidden to give reasons for its verdict. No one really knows much of anything about how juries behave or how they operate.

In 1952 the Chicago University Law School set out to learn; and one of the ways it went about learning was to put a tape recorder in the jury room in six civil cases which were on trial in the United States District Court in Kansas. This was in the spring of 1954. Permission had been obtained from the judge, from all the parties, from their lawyers, from everyone except the jurors themselves. The jurors were not told till later. There was a great stir about it. Opinions differed; and no more juries were tapped.

I take the obscurantist position that this was an outrage, but that is not the point I want to make, which is this. You cannot observe the jury's deliberations without changing its character. The jurors don't have to know they are being observed and what they say recorded. They need only fear that they may be observed to talk and act quite differently. A jury that thinks it is being observed is as much interfered with as an atom that is being observed.

I don't know whether the atom behaves better or worse under observation. I don't know that empathy goes that far. But I do believe that a jury that knows or even thinks it may be under scrutiny is not a jury, but some other kind of tribunal.

There are some things that are best done in secret. There are some that cannot be done otherwise. I wonder if we should now have a Constitution or even be United; I wonder what we would be, if the deliberations of our Constitutional Convention in 1787 had not been secret. I may add that

Madison's notes of the proceedings were not published during his lifetime, and not until 1840, when Congress ordered the publication of all of Madison's papers from the original manuscripts on deposit with the Department of State.

❋ 77 ❋

"POL: You go to seek the Lord Hamlet; there he is.

ROS: (To Polonius) God save you, sir! (Exit Polonius.)

GUIL: My honoured lord!

ROS: My most dear lord!

HAM: My excellent good friends! How dost thou, Guildenstern? Ah, Rosencrantz! Good lads, how do you both?

ROS: As the indifferent children of the earth.

GUIL: Happy, in that we are not over-happy; On Fortune's cap we are not the very button.

HAM: Nor the soles of her shoe?

ROS: Neither, my lord.

HAM: Then you live about her waist, or in the middle of her favours?

GUIL: Faith, her privates we.

HAM: In the secret parts of Fortune? O, most true; she is a strumpet. What's the news?

ROS: None, my lord, but that the world's grown honest.

HAM: Then is doomsday near. But your news is not true. Let me question more in particular. What have you, my good friends, deserved at the hands of Fortune, that she sends you to prison hither?

GUIL: Prison, my lord!

HAM: *Denmark's a prison.*

ROS: *Then is the world one.*

HAM: *A goodly one; in which there are many confines, wards, and dungeons, Denmark being one o' the worst.*

ROS: *We think not so, my lord.*

HAM: *Why, then 'tis none to you; for there is nothing either good or bad, but thinking makes it so: to me it is a prison.*

ROS: *Why, then your ambition makes it one; 'tis too narrow for your mind.*

HAM: *O God, I could be bounded in a nut-shell and count myself a king of infinite space, were it not that I have bad dreams."*

HAMLET WAS reading. Polonius had interrupted him, and now, as Polonius was leaving and Hamlet about to go back to his book, his two friends, Rosencrantz and Guildenstern, came in and interrupted him again. The book was Florio's translation of Montaigne, and Hamlet had just started chapter 40.

Let me say that Florio's translation of Montaigne came out in 1603. The part of the scene I have quoted is not in the First Quarto, in 1603. It is in the Second Quarto, which was published in 1604, just after Shakespear had read Florio. Hamlet was reading this:

"Men (saith an ancient Greeke sentence) are tormented by the opinions they have of things, and not by things themselves. It were a great conquest for the ease of our miserable humane condition, if any man could establish every where this true proposition. For if evils have no entrance into us, but by our judgement, it seemeth that it lieth in our power, either to contemne or turne them to our good. If things yeeld themselves unto our mercie, why should we not have the fruition of them, or apply them to our advantage? If that which we call evill and torment, be neither torment, nor evill, but that our fancie only gives it that qualitie, it is in us to change it: and having the choice of it, if none compell us, we are very fooles, to bandy for that partie, which is irkesome unto us: and to give infirmities, indigence, and contempt, a sharpe and ill taste, if we may give them a good: And if fortune simply affoord us the matter, it lieth in us to give it the forme. Now that which we terme evill, is not so of it selfe, or at least, such as it is, that it depends of us to give it another taste, and another countenance (for all comes to one) let us see whether it can be maintained."

"And count myself a king of infinite space," Hamlet said. When Thoreau went to jail, rather than pay his poll tax, he said, "I saw that if there was a wall of stone between me and my townsmen, there was a still more difficult one to climb or break through before they could get to be as free as I was. I did not for a moment feel confined, and the walls seemed a great waste of stone and mortar. I felt as if I alone of all my townsmen had paid my tax."

And some readers of the *Atlantic Monthly* may remember my verse about Dunbar Lockwood's Siamese cat:

> "These are the things I like best to do:
> Most of the time it is loving you,
> And taking pains I shouldn't show it,
> Partly because I know you know it.
> But after you I love the sun,
> And when I can I watch it run
> Across the sky from pole to pole,
> Like some great mouse from hole to hole.
> And when I'm bored with that, I play
> With you. At times I hear you say
> You *play* with me. Cats know
> Men like to think that this is so.
> And since you are my god-elect
> I shouldn't want you to suspect
> It was the other way about,
> Just as at night I shut you in
> When you believe you let me out."

I must add that the cat died, and then this verse, also in the *Atlantic Monthly*:

> "Men die. A bishop lays their bones,
> By book and candle, under stones.
> Cats die. The only pomp they're paid
> Is the rude ritual of the spade.
> He smiles. As if the things we cherish,
> Either way, could ever perish."

❊ 78 ❊

"For Spirits, when they please,
Can either sex assume, or both. . . ."

I DO NOT pretend to know as much as Milton did
about Spirits, but I see nothing remarkable about
a Spirit sharing something of each sex as well as
being wholly either. Doors are not always either
open or shut. It is a mistaken notion that you can't
eat your cake and have it too. This is true only
when you are hungry enough or greedy enough to
eat it all up. The more you eat, the less you have,
true. The less you eat, the more you have, is equally
true. Yet the moralists insist that we must either
eat it or have it. What absolute knaves they are!
They are telling us, in the words of the old French
song,

"Rempli ton verre vide!
Vide ton verre plein!
Je ne puis souffrir dans ta main
Un verre ni vide ni plein."

May we not sit quietly at our table, or stand
agreeably together at the bar, with a half-empty

glass in our hands, secure in the certain knowledge that it is also half-full?

There are two different kinds of questions. One is the kind that must be answered either one way or the other. Then the acceptance of one is a rejection of the other. The other kind of question calls for quite a different kind of answer, a more-or-less instead of an either-or. It is an important difference, because it is easier to think in terms of black or white, right or wrong, all or none. Moralists are eager to set good against evil, vice against virtue, although there are higher and lower levels in both heaven and hell. So we are pressed into believing that all momentous decisions are either-ors, and scarcely, if ever, more-or-lesses.

It is not only the moralists that oppress us and pester us. The apostles of simplicity are as fanatical as the apostles of virtue. Simple things are harder to understand, and yet simple questions are easier to answer and simple decisions easier to make. We ask a jury or a judge simply to decide for or against us. But we know that this simple either-or is as crude as it is decisive. So we ask the court to ameliorate its decision, with an obeisance toward the more-or-less, by fixing the damages or the sentence. The story that Alexander cut the Gordian knot, Tarn says, is "certainly untrue."

And sometimes I wonder, with some concern, what Solomon would have done with the baby, had neither woman spoken up.

✻ 79 ✻

"*It is established by experience that softness and indulgence toward yourself and hardness toward others is one and the same vice.*"

WOULD LA BRUYÈRE agree that the converse, hardness toward yourself and indulgence toward others, were likewise one and the same virtue?

❀ 80 ❀

"There are indeed cases where the real choice is between two extremes, either of them being in fact
better than anything intermediate—a curious exception to Aristotle's preference for the mean. The
classical example is, of course, that of the Caudine
Forks where Cato advised that the entrapped Sam-
ites should either be all killed so as to subjugate the
tribe, or let go unharmed and thereby made friends,
but situations of this kind are constantly recurring
in public life and in business affairs. A factory with
an inadequate plant, machinery out of date, and
short of assets is faced by the alternative of raising
new capital or going out of business, either being
better than struggling along, constantly losing
money and rolling up debt until bankruptcy is inevitable. A university may contain a department
which under existing conditions does not, and cannot, do satisfactory work, which is rather a snare
than a benefit to the students that enter it, which
cannot be made really useful without a drain upon
the valuable parts of the institution, and yet where
pride makes its abandonment difficult. In these examples hesitation or delay is the least desirable
course to pursue. Such cases usually result from

164

misfortune, both alternatives being objectionable. They often occur unexpectedly and require rapid decision. Therefore they are peculiarly difficult, and people will disagree about the wisdom of the decision; but they often lead to great success or failure."

I READ the following in the Alsops' column the other day about the National Security Council:

"In the first place, the Council has tended to become an instrument not for reaching hard decisions, but for reaching the lowest common denominator of indecision. President Eisenhower, as in the matter of Quemoy and Matsu, will occasionally take matters into his own hands and overrule the NSC. But like President Truman before him, and for understandable reasons, he heartily dislikes 'split papers.' Thus the NSC system generates a heavy pressure for unanimity at all costs.

"Unanimity often boils down to generalities— many NSC papers these days are reliably reported to consist of meaninglessness couched in impeccable governmentese, and nothing else at all. And when real decisions cannot be avoided, unanimity is almost always achieved simply by splitting the difference. Do we, for example, make a major effort to overtake the Soviet lead in missile development, or is it more important to balance the budget? The NSC splits the difference. The missile effort is stepped up somewhat, but not enough to throw

165

the budget out of whack—or to catch up with the Soviets. This way of splitting is about as useful as building a bridge halfway across a river."

Sir Oliver Franks saw a great deal of President Truman through the six years 1946–1952, and in his review of Truman's memoirs in *The Listener*, Franks says, "Mr. Truman, as President, had extraordinary powers of decision. This is not a common gift. The capacity to decide is rare. It is very rare indeed when the problems are on a world scale and full of dangers. General Marshall had a favorite saying which he once used when I was discussing an issue with him and his advisers in the State Department. 'Gentlemen,' he said, 'don't fight the question. Decide it.' The temptation is always to fight the difficult decisions, to fight them off. So often all the possible courses seem risky and unpleasant. It is not easy to get the facts clear or to foresee what the consequences of particular decisions will be. Taking decisions on foreign affairs in times of crisis is hard work for men of great courage. Mr. Truman has this capacity to decide, with all the endowment of moral courage and sheer hard work that it implies."

❊ 81 ❊

"Nature has put us so well into the middle that if we change one side of the scale we change the other too. This makes me think there are springs in our head which are so disposed that what touches one touches also the other."

PASCAL CROSSED out this passage, but I can't help wondering if it does not explain my own liability to give the diametrically wrong answer when I have correctly stated the issue. Often, if I simply reverse the answer, I find it is what I meant. Likewise—for it must be the same failing—I find it difficult to understand simple alternatives, such as: if this, then that; if that, then this. The words *former* and *latter* mean nothing to me. The springs in my head are so connected, so disposed, that when a thought touches one it touches its contrary at the same time. This is obscure to me, and perhaps, if I were a Pascal, I'd cross it all out.

On the other hand, I can tell a sieve from a colander as well as the next man; or night from day —dusk, yes; but in the words of the old indictments for burglary, " 'twixt dog and wolf." So too with those obscure differences that are less distinct than their respective consequences. They tell me that Latin has two words for *or*, *aut* when the difference is either sharp or consequential, *vel* when it is neither.

❈ 82 ❈

"No, Cassius; for the eye sees not itself,
But by reflection, by some other things."

Nor, for that matter, does the mind. For, unless you are two people, how can you be conscious of yourself?

I can make no sense out of Descartes' *Cogito, ergo sum*, unless there are two egos, one to think and the other to be. And if there are two, then the fact that one thinks proves nothing about the existence of the other.

We are conscious of ourselves only by reflection from other things. William James said, "Many philosophers, however, hold that the reflective consciousness of the self is essential to the cognitive function of thought. They hold that a thought, in order to know a thing at all, must expressly distinguish between the thing and its own self." James did not agree. He said, "This is a perfectly wanton assumption, and not the faintest shadow of reason exists for supposing it true. As well might I contend that I cannot dream without dreaming that I dream, swear without swearing that I swear, deny without denying that I deny, as maintain that I cannot know without knowing that I know."

All we know about ourselves, all we ever can know is our reflection in other things. For, unless we are two people, we can never look directly at ourselves. And so we do our best when we are not aware that there may be more than one of us.

And yet:

"*Momentous to himself, as I to me,*
Hath each man been that ever woman bore;
Once, in a lightning-flash of sympathy,
I felt this truth, an instant, and no more."

❊ 83 ❊

"*Sometimes I pose, but sometimes I pose as posing.*"

This is the preface, the whole preface, to Stella Benson's novel, *I Pose*. And the last line of the book is, "Yes, I pose of course. But the question is —how deep may a pose extend?"

169

If Hazlitt is right, all the way down and through. "Man is a make-believe animal," Hazlitt asserted, "He is never so truly himself as when he is acting a part."

Which leads us to the next question: What sort of an animal would man be if he couldn't pose?

And the next after that is: How could he pose if he wasn't capable of knowing he was posing?

❈ 84 ❈

"A state such that if a small modification different from that which will otherwise occur is imposed upon a system, a reaction will at once appear, tending toward the conditions that would have existed if the modification had not been impressed."

THIS STATEMENT has been plucking at the sleeve of my understanding for a long time. I have never been able to brush it off. Nor quite understand it. My mind has teetered between neglecting it as trite and revering it as a piece of inscrutable wisdom.

I got it from Lawrence J. Henderson, and you will find it in his book on Pareto. Henderson was talking about social systems and he gives a few examples of this equilibrium: the recovery from short wars, from not too serious epidemics, and from lesser catastrophes. Elsewhere, talking about Hippocrates, he referred it to a state of health in the patient.

There is also a remark by Machiavelli—which I think I must also have got from Henderson and which has also long plucked at my sleeve: "Republics have a longer life and enjoy better fortune than principalities, because they can profit by their greater internal diversity. They are the better able to meet emergencies." I think this comes from Machiavelli's *Discourses on Livy*, not from *The Prince*.

It is a common enough observation that a small modification of a stable system has no permanent consequences. You can jump out of a warm bed into a cold shower, and yet your temperature remains constant. President Eisenhower's heart attack gave the stock market only a temporary snub.

Is it worth while wondering about the reason for this state of equilibrium? Or is it metaphysical? I ran on a passage in Stuart Hampshire's book on Spinoza, which allowed me to think that this was the answer:

"This is part of the meaning of the all-important Proposition VII of Part III of the *Ethics*: 'The endeavour (*conatus*) wherewith each thing endeavours to persist in its own being is nothing more than the actual essence of the thing itself.' The greater the power of self-maintenance of the particular

171

thing in the face of external causes, the greater reality it has, and the more clearly it can be distinguished as having a definite nature and individuality. Within Spinoza's definitions, therefore, it is a tautology that every finite thing, including a human being, endeavours to preserve itself and to increase its power of self-maintenance; the *conatus* is a necessary feature of everything in Nature, because this tendency to self-maintenance is involved in the definition of what it is to be a distinct and identifiable thing."

This is certainly metaphysical enough: "essence," "its own being," "the thing itself," "the greater reality"; and tautological at that. But there remains the fact. Things do recover and recuperate in a somewhat mysterious manner. It may be mathematical, for all I know. It may have something to do with feedbacks and re-entrant causes, and the way of guided missiles and calculating machines. I am too far from knowing even to be curious. And yet I wish someone would tell me one thing. Is it true that the more complex and the more diversified a system is, the more efficacious is this recuperative and restorative principle? I want very much to believe that Machiavelli was right.

And here, I think, lies the answer. This notion of equilibrium is true of our understanding of things. Our beliefs, our opinions, our attitudes have their own equilibrium, which may or may not be shared by the things themselves. It was my misguided attempt to apply it to things instead of to my understanding of them that kept me teetering between reverence and neglect.

We try to content ourselves with satisfactory thoughts. When they do not get along with our experiences, we have to compose and reconcile their differences, just as any host will do his best to give his guests an agreeable evening. We are hospitable mentally as well as socially. Hospitable; and sometimes convivial.

❁ 85 ❁

"The totality of our so-called knowledge or beliefs, from the most casual matters of geography and history to the profoundest laws of atomic physics or even of pure mathematics and logic, is a man-made fabric which impinges on experience only along the edges. Or, to change the figure, total science is like a field of force whose boundary conditions are experience. A conflict with experience at the periphery occasions readjustments in the interior of the field. Truth values have to be redistributed over some of our statements. Re-evaluation of some statements entails re-evaluation of others, because of their logical interconnections—the logical laws being in turn simply certain further statements of the system, certain further elements of the field. Having re-evaluated one statement we must re-evaluate some others, which may be statements logically connected with the first or may be the statements of logical connections themselves. But the total field is so underdetermined by its boundary conditions, experience, that there is much latitude of choice as to what statements to re-evaluate in the light of any single contrary experience. No particular experiences are linked with any particular statements in

174

the interior of the field, except indirectly through considerations of equilibrium affecting the field as a whole."

Here is our equilibrium. But look where Quine is leading us and how far. Consider what happens to things, things physical and things mythical, everything on the other end of our relation to them.

"As an empiricist," Quine goes on to say, "I continue to think of the conceptual scheme of science as a tool, ultimately, for predicting future experience in the light of past experience. Physical objects are conceptually imported into the situation as convenient intermediaries—not by definition in terms of experience, but simply as irreducible posits comparable, epistemologically, to the gods of Homer. For my part I do, *qua* lay physicist, believe in physical objects and not in Homer's gods; and I consider it a scientific error to believe otherwise. But in point of epistemological footing the physical objects and the gods differ only in degree and not in kind. Both sorts of entities enter our conception only as cultural posits. The myth of physical objects is epistemologically superior to most in that it has proved more efficacious than other myths as a device for working a manageable structure into the flux of experience."

Now watch abstractions follow concrete assertions into the pot, even those we are most sure of, certainties following certitudes, mathematics and mythologies hand in hand.

"Physical objects, small and large, are not the only posits. Forces are another example; and indeed we are told nowadays that the boundary between energy and matter is obsolete. Moreover, the abstract entities which are the substance of mathematics—ultimately classes and classes of classes and so on up—are another posit in the same spirit. Epistemologically these are myths on the same footing with physical objects and gods, neither better nor worse except for differences in the degree to which they expedite our dealings with sense experiences.

"The over-all algebra of rational and irrational numbers is underdetermined by the algebra of rational numbers, but is smoother and more convenient; and it includes the algebra of rational numbers as a jagged or gerrymandered part. Total science, mathematical and natural and human, is similarly but more extremely underdetermined by experience. The edge of the system must be kept squared with experience, the rest, with all its elaborate myths or fictions, has as its objective the simplicity of laws."

As you see, this is the tree of knowledge, swayed and buffeted by the winds of new doctrine, sometimes stirred to its very roots, and finally either torn up by a hurricane or cut down for a street widening.

❋ 86 ❋

"But, alas!
I am as true as truth's simplicity,
And simpler than the infancy of truth."

THERE IS a Troilus in most scientists' attitude toward natural laws. Bertrand Russell says, "It is customary to add to the postulate that there are natural laws the explicit or tacit proviso that they must be *simple*. This, however, is both vague and teleological. It is not clear what is meant by 'simplicity,' and there can be no priori reason for expecting laws to be simple except benevolence on the part of Providence toward men of science."

Why we admire simplicity and why we want to make things seem simple, is not at all clear. It is not that simple notions are the easier to understand. The familiar, however rococo and complicated, is easier to understand. Even Bacon rejected Kepler. You and I may think we understand Newton. We know we do not understand Einstein's simplification. I am referring, mark you, to understanding as the completed process, as a satisfaction of understanding. If you take understanding as a process, on the march and in motion, it is another matter. But to reach a satisfactory understanding of something may very well become the harder, the more simply it is stated. This is so not only in science. It is true of mathematics. Take the idea of zero, or the square root of minus one, or the inscrutable notions of infinity. It is equally true of all grand generalizations, in poetry or in ethics. Do you understand the Golden Rule? Or the statement that impressed T. S. Eliot, "Ripeness is all"? Or Dante's statement that seems to Eliot to be "literally true," *"la sua voluntade é nostra pace"*? The simple statements are the hardest to understand, and sometimes simply inexplicable.

When we find something simply and clearly stated and wholly intelligible, it is only because the author has expressed our ideas better than we had been able to express them ourselves. We are pleased because the author agrees with us. And why not?

There is something exasperating about the notion of simplicity. By rights it ought to reflect itself, and itself be simple, but it's not. A mathematician or a scientist, I know, may find peace in saying that a thing is the simpler only for having the fewer independent variables in its make-up. This is so, but it does not give me any comfort. It is just those things that have the fewest independent variables that come down hardest on our understanding, until finally if we think we have succeeded in reducing something to a unit—as we once thought we had with the atom—or to a totality in itself, we find that we are crossing the frontier into mysticism. All we achieve by reducing the number of variables is an increase in the number of what we take as constants, not an increase of our understanding of the whole thing.

I have heard it suggested that the virtue of simplicity lies in its power to make things credible, because it is easier to believe simple things than complicated or compounded things. I don't know about that, but I suspect credibility is a theological virtue. An omnipotent God is the simplest solution of almost every problem, except, to be sure, Himself. And does not this suggestion confuse belief with understanding and so beg the question?

There remains the steep fact that there are many obviously simple things I do not understand. So many that I wonder if it may not be their very simplicity that makes them unintelligible to me.

And yet complexities irk us, and our understanding keeps moving toward further simplicities. We are continually shaken out of each new ease into a further simplicity. Sometimes it is the insolent behavior of experience, but not always. There are many to whom comfort brings no ease. Their doubts and disbeliefs, which they cherish as dearly as we do our convictions and our certitudes, nag at our complacence.

❋ 87 ❋

"The aim of science is to seek the simplest explanations of complex facts. We are apt to fall into the error of thinking that the facts are simple because simplicity is the goal of our quest. The guiding motto in the life of every natural philosopher should be, 'Seek simplicity and distrust it!' "

Whitehead may be right, and simplicity may be the goal of science and not simply a human need, the Old Troilus in us along with the Old Adam.

But I wonder. Do we know just what we mean by this simplicity which is the goal of science? Might it not be just neatness, or more precisely, just a sense of tidiness? Or even something grander and more impressive, like elegance, or even beauty?

Quine has said something which makes me think he will agree.

"Elegance, conceptual economy, also enters as an objective. But this virtue, engaging though it is, is secondary—sometimes in one way and sometimes in another. Elegance can make the difference between a psychologically manageable conceptual scheme and one that is too unwieldy for our poor minds to cope with effectively. When this happens, elegance is simply a means to the end of a pragmatically acceptable conceptual scheme. But elegance also enters as an end in itself—and quite properly so as long as it remains secondary in another respect; namely, as long as it is appealed to only in choices where the pragmatic standard prescribes no contrary decision. Where elegance doesn't matter, we may and shall, as poets, pursue elegance for elegance's sake."

I remember Harlow Shapley once telling me that on opening a book on mathematics he was sometimes moved by the same emotions he had when he entered a great cathedral.

"Beauty is truth, truth beauty. . ." I wonder if we may not be able to make sense out of this if we take truth pragmatically. Thoreau jotted down in his journal, "Beauty is a finer utility whose end we do not see." I think both Quine and Shapley would agree with Thoreau.

Henri Poincaré agreed, because he said, "It may be surprising to see emotional sensibility invoked a propos of mathematical demonstrations which, it would seem, can interest only the intellect. This would be to forget the feeling of mathematical beauty, of the harmony of numbers and forms, of geometric elegance. This is a true esthetic feeling that all real mathematicians know, and surely it belongs to emotional sensibility."

Hadamard, who quotes this from Poincaré, adds:

"The guide we must confide in is that sense of scientific beauty, that special esthetic sensibility, the importance of which he has pointed out.

"As Renan also curiously notices, there is a scientific taste just as there is a literary or artistic one; and that taste, according to individuals, may be more or less sure.

"Concerning the fruitfulness of the future result, about which, strictly speaking, we most often do not know anything in advance, that sense of beauty can inform us and I cannot see anything else allowing us to foresee. At least, contesting that would seem to me to be a mere question of words. Without knowing anything further, we *feel* that such a direction of investigation is worth following; we feel that the question *in itself* deserves interest, that its solution will be of some value for science, whether it permits further applications or not. Everybody is free to call or not to call that a feeling of beauty. This is undoubtedly the way the Greek geometers thought when they investigated the ellipse, because there is no other conceivable way."

✳ 88 ✳

"And so you are dragged on by consistency. It never occurs to you that a thing may be self-consistent and yet false. If a man says twice five is seven and you take his word for it without checking the sum, he will naturally deduce that four times five is fourteen, and so on ad libitum. This is the way that weird geometry proceeds. It sets before beginners certain strange assumptions, and insists on their granting the existence of inconceivable things, such as points having no parts, lines without breadth, and so on, builds on these rotten foundations a superstructure equally rotten, and pretends to go on to a demonstration which is true, though it starts from premises which are false."

LUCIAN IS talking about rival schools of philosophy, and he goes on to tell a Stoic, "Just so you, when you have granted the principles of any school, believe in the deductions from them, and take their consistency, false as it is, for a guarantee of truth."

This is all very well, but I'm not sure that Lucian's own foot isn't slipping into the same hole toward which he is dragging the Stoic. For consistency has no more to do with falsity than it has with truth. Consistency is a characteristic of something that is to be used or applied, and it is a virtue only when, and only so far as, it makes the thing more intelligible or more useful. It has only a pragmatic—morganatic—relation with truth.

For me the best example is in the law. The law, all of it—statutes, regulations, precedents, opinions —should be as self-consistent as possible, just so that every relevant provision may be immediately and readily available for application to the instant case. I cannot think of any other reason why the law should be consistent, unless it be to make the law easier for law students to understand.

The parties in a case have a right to the benefit of all of the law. You have a right to have imposed on you nothing less than, nothing short of, the whole of the law relevant to your case. Consistency makes what is relevant available. It's another sort of neatness.

Nor does the truth or falsity of these notions offer anything of interest. Here we pick up the general rule that the more general a notion is, the less its usefulness depends on its truth. The more you come down to particulars, the more their truth becomes all-important. Take what Lucian is talking about: points without parts, lines without breadth, etc., none of which makes sense, far less what we can call true. They are none the less useful.

Tobias Dantzig quotes Nietzsche:

"We hold mere falsity no ground for rejecting a

judgment. The issue is: to what extent has the conception preserved and furthered the life of the race? The falsest conceptions—and to these belong our synthetic judgments *a priori*—are also those which are the most indispensable. Without his logical fictions, without measuring reality in a fictitious absolute and immutable world, without the perpetual counterfeiting of the universe by number, man could not continue to live. The renunciation of all false judgment would mean a renunciation, a negation of life."

Dantzig's comment is: "The criterion of validity for any illusion is a *post factum* and sometimes a *post mortem* judgment. Those that preserve and further the life of the race thrive and grow, and thus earn their right to reality; those that are harmful or useless eventually find their way to the textbooks on metaphysics and theology, and there they stay. So they, too, do not die in vain."

✻ 89 ✻

"*I incline to think that Nature first made the things themselves as she best liked, and afterwards framed the reason of man capable of conceiving (though not without great pains) some part of her secrets.*"

Bᴜᴛ ᴡᴇ, and our reason with us, are part of Nature. And how can one part comprehend another part? Were we outside it, we could understand it no better, for outside of Nature, we should have nothing in common with her.

Schrödinger has suggested the analogy of the poet putting himself into his own epic, specifically Homer portraying himself as Demodocus, the blind bard who sang to Alcinoös and Odysseus in the *Odyssey*. But the poet writes his own epic. We did not make Nature. Or did we, at least so much of her as we understand?

❊ 90 ❊

"Perfect plainness of speech."

I CAN SYMPATHIZE with those who say, 'Put it into plain, simple English,' especially when they protest against the empty formalism of loading discourse with pseudo-learned words. But to restrict thinking to the patterns merely of English, and especially to those patterns which represent the acme of plainness in English, is to lose a power of thought which, once lost, can never be regained. It is the 'plainest' English which contains the greatest number of unconscious assumptions about nature. This is the trouble with schemes like Basic English, in which an eviscerated British English, with its concealed premises working harder than ever, is to be fobbed off on an unsuspecting world as the substance of pure Reason itself. We handle even our plain English with much greater effect if we direct it from the vantage point of a multilingual awareness. For this reason I believe that those who envision a future world speaking only one tongue, whether English, German, Russian, or any other, hold a misguided ideal and would do the evolution of the human mind the greatest disservice. Western culture has made, through language, a provisional analysis of reality and, without correctives, holds resolutely to that analysis as final. The only correctives lie in all those other tongues which by aeons of independent evolution have arrived at different, but equally logical, provisional analyses." So Benjamin Lee Whorf.

Quine asks, "How much of our science is merely contributed by language and how much is a genuine reflection of reality?"

And Quine replies, "Certainly we are in a predicament if we try to answer the question; for to answer the question we must talk about the world as well as about language, and to talk about the world we must already impose upon the world some conceptual scheme peculiar to our own special language.

"Yet we must not leap to the fatalistic conclusion that we are stuck with the conceptual scheme that we grew up in. We can change it bit by bit, plank by plank, though meanwhile there is nothing to carry us along but the evolving conceptual scheme itself. The philosopher's task was well compared by Neurath to that of a mariner who must rebuild his ship on the open sea.

"We can improve our conceptual scheme, our philosophy, bit by bit while continuing to depend on it for support; but we cannot detach ourselves from it and compare it objectively with an unconceptualized reality. Hence it is meaningless, I suggest, to inquire into the absolute correctness of a conceptual scheme as a mirror of reality. Our standard for appraising basic changes of conceptual scheme must be, not a realistic standard of correspondence to reality, but a pragmatic standard. Concepts are language, and the purpose of concepts and of language is efficacy in communication and in prediction. Such is the ultimate duty of language, science, and philosophy, and it is in relation to that duty that a conceptual scheme has finally to be appraised."

❋ 91 ❋

"We cannot well do without our sins; they are the highway of our virtue." So Thoreau.

"The web of our life is of a mingled yarn, good and ill together. Our virtues would be proud, if our faults whipped them not, and our crimes would despair, if they were not cherished by our virtues." So Shakespear.

I wish our virtues would lay off our vices, leave them alone, neither cherish them, nor use them as a highway.

Why can't we now and then park off the highway, or even picnic in the woods? I never wholly agreed with the Countess that the trouble with doing your duty was that it unfitted you for doing anything else. And yet there is no doubt that ethics crowd us. We very much need a sort of a wild wish sanctuary and picnic area, where we are free to be ourselves.

Max Radin thought this one of the functions of the law. "Not only what we ought to do or not to do, but what we may do if we choose or leave undone if we prefer is the business of the law."

❃ 92 ❃

"*I say unto you, that likewise joy shall be in Heaven over one sinner that repenteth, more than over ninety and nine just persons, which need no repentance.*"

A MOST UNFORTUNATE remark. It has brought glory to reformed drunks, spiritual luxury to Oxford Groupers, and credibility to ex-Communists. How far, and why, a sense of sin should be necessary to salvation are questions I cannot even understand, far less offer to answer. How such an astringent mind as Thoreau's came to write in his *Journal*, "We cannot well do without our sins; they are the highway of our virtue," is beyond me. All I can say is, he was young, only twenty-five (March 22, 1842). Why does Toynbee deplore our lack of a sense of sin and find "a favorable omen" in "the shock tactics of the so-called 'Oxford Groups' "?

It is right and proper that we should be angry with ourselves. As a matter of fact, it is usually ourselves that we are angry with when we blame others, and always when we kick what has tripped us. But why should we be so proud of being sorry? William James was right: "Even repentance and remorse, affections which come in the character of ministers of good, may be but sickly and relaxing impulses. The best repentance is to up and act for righteousness, and forget that you ever had relations with sin." And James quotes Spinoza, who condemned repentance as a "deleterious and evil passion." The sense of sin, Whitehead told Lucien Price, was "the worst blight that ever fell on man." I suggest that guilt and sin are only a fear of the past.

It is doubly unfortunate, because there is so much truth in the remark, once it is stripped of the sense of sin, that one of the signs of greatness is a willingness to admit you were mistaken. "My brethren, by the bowels of Christ I beseech you, bethink you that you may be mistaken."

I don't know whether Cromwell was beseeching the House of Commons or the General Assembly of the Church of Scotland, nor whether these were his exact words, but the point is, Cromwell appealed to the authority of Christ, and he must have

191

had, he may have had, I like to think he had, in mind this passage I have quoted from Luke. If so, I think he read it more correctly than we translate it. For Jesus did not quite say "repent" or "repentance." He used a much milder word, *"metanoia,"* which comes more nearly to mean only a change of mind, with or without regrets. The word for repentance would be *"metameleia."* Anyhow, I don't see any sense of sin in the Gospels. Wasn't it Saint Paul and Saint Augustine that brought that to us?

❊ 93 ❊

"I believe it is a sign of a healthy conscience in a country if they are determined to avenge crime."

THIS IS what Lord Goddard, the Lord Chief Justice, said in the House of Lords as he cast his vote against the abolition of the death penalty. And I suppose the old pagan is quite right. *Que Messieurs les Assassins commencent!* But I'd like very much to know just what the Chief Justice means by "a healthy conscience."

I think I know what this statement means. I am not at all sure about the other, which is repeated in Matthew and in Mark. But this one in the 17th chapter means to me that saving your own soul can be selfish business, so much so that it may defeat its purpose.

Fiat justitia et ruant coeli. But if you are Atlas? Will you let it drop, will you let the heavens fall, when it is your job to keep them up? A physician may not tell his patient "the truth" in order to save his own conscience. He saves himself at his patient's expense. And so likewise a lawyer, too pious to incur a lie to protect his client's confidence, blurts out the truth, his client's truth.

"Thou villain, thou art full of piety."

❋ 97 ❋

"The true philosopher laughs at philosophy."

THIS IS the climax of the fragment of Pascal I quoted earlier. I don't think it is as cryptic as it appears to be.

Brunschvicg points out that Pascal got it from Montaigne, from whom he got so much else; and so reluctantly, and a little resentfully, as I think comes clear in his interview with Monsieur de Saci. What Montaigne said was this: "One of the ancients, when he was reproached for making a profession of philosophy, in spite of his not holding philosophy in great account, said that this was to be a true philosopher."

Which of the ancients this was we do not know, but Pascal adopted it in another fragment:

"You are not to think of Plato and Aristotle as always dressed in their academic gowns. They were good fellows, and like other people, they laughed with their friends. They were enjoying themselves when they wrote their Laws and Politics. They wrote for the fun of it. It was the least philosophic and the least serious part of their lives. The most philosophic was to live simply and serenely. What they wrote about politics were rules for an insane asylum; and if they made it appear to be a matter of great importance, it's because they knew that the madmen to whom they were speaking thought they were kings and emperors. They were laying down the principles by which their madness might, so far as possible, be moderated."

Hans Zinsser marked a similar passage in Unamuno's *The Tragic Sense of Life*:

"If a philosopher is not a man, he is anything but a philosopher; he is above all a pedant, and a pedant is a caricature of a man. The cultivation of any branch of science—of chemistry, of physics, of geometry, of philology—may be a work of differentiated specialization, and even so only within very narrow limits and restrictions; but philosophy, like poetry, is a work of integration and synthesis, or else it is merely pseudo-philosophical erudition."

❋ 98 ❋

"That the essence of faith lies in a positive response to something that calls out a 'yes' from our whole nature, I believe to be profoundly true. It is not even rightly expressed as a 'decision' to believe (a term often used in such discussions). I believe that Calvin was right when he saw, perhaps in a distorted way, that if you had to decide whether to believe or not, you did not really have faith. When faith is present, it holds with a sense of inevitability. You cannot choose whether to give or withhold consent any more than a trained musician can choose whether or not to play the right note."

THERE ARE two parallel passages in Justice Holmes, one in his "Ideals and Doubts" in 1915, the other in what he wrote on "Natural Law" in 1918.

"When I say that a thing is true," Holmes said, "I mean that I cannot help believing it. I am stating an experience as to which there is no choice. But as there are many things that I cannot help doing that the universe can, I do not venture to assume that my inabilities in the way of thought are inabilities of the universe. I therefore define the truth as the system of my limitations and leave absolute truth to those who are better equipped."

"If, as I have suggested elsewhere, the truth may be defined as the system of my (intellectual) limitations, what gives it objectivity is the fact that I find my fellow-man to a greater or less extent (never wholly) subject to the same *Can't Helps*."

The point of agreement between Miss Dorothy Emmet—it was from her book, *The Nature of Metaphysical Thinking*, that I first quoted—and Justice Holmes is the compulsive nature of their beliefs. Miss Emmet finds "a sense of the inevitable" in what she believes. Holmes "can't help" believing what he believes. What each believes is beside the point, but what are we to think of faith in faith itself? What do you say of a creed that breaks off after the two words, "I believe. . . ."

Reinhold Niebuhr has said, "The 'unknown God' of Americans seems to be faith itself," and Will Herberg, after quoting this, goes on to say, "What Americans believe in when they are religious is, as we have already had occasion to see, religion itself. Of course, religious Americans speak of God and Christ, but what they seem to regard as really redemptive is primarily religion, the 'positive' attitude of *believing*. It is this faith in faith, this religion that makes religion its own object, that is the outstanding characteristic of contemporary American religiosity. Daniel Poling's formula: 'I began saying in the morning two words, "I believe"—those two words *with nothing added* (emphasis not in original) may be taken as the classic expression of this aspect of American faith."

No wonder that there is nothing inevitable about such a belief. I can't help thinking that it must be very difficult to believe in nothing in particular. It is the Indian rope trick. It is like a bare flagpole. Or else it's like falling in love with love, or art for art's sake—or any other version of two mirrors facing each other.

❊ 99 ❊

"Asked: whether she knew that she was in the grace of God,

"Answered: If I am not, may God please to put me in it; and if I am, may God please to keep me in it;

"And she said that if she knew she was not in the grace of God, she would be the most sorrowful person in the world (la plus dolente du monde);

"Said also, if she was in sin, that the voice would not come to her. And wished that everyone understood it as well as she did herself."

IT WAS the third day of Joan's trial, Saturday, February 24, 1431. In the vestry chamber at the end of the great court of the chateau in Rouen. The Bishop of Beauvais was presiding. Some fifty persons, mostly ecclesiastics, were there. Joan was nineteen. She had no attorney, no friend. It was Lent and she had been fasting since noon of the day before.

Was there ever a better answer on cross-examination? If Joan had said, Yes, I am in a state of grace, it would have been a presumption of her own salvation. If she said, No, that would be a confession.

I wonder how long she paused, or perhaps hesitated, before she added how sorrowful she would be, were she not; and then how long a silence before she referred to her voice. She had just been testifying that she had been woken by her voice the day before. At first, before she was awake, the voice had said something she had not understood. But then, when she was awake, the voice told her to answer boldly (*hardiment*).

Indeed she had answered boldly. She went on to tell the Bishop, "You say that you are my judge. Take good care of what you do, for in truth I am sent by God, and you are putting yourself in great danger." And when she was pressed to say more about this voice, she told the Bishop that the voices had said she should tell certain things to the King and not to him.

Joan's voices advised her to answer boldly, because they knew she'd be a good witness.

There have been two comments on this answer of hers: "*Si je n'y suis, Dieu m'y veuille mettre; et si j'y suis, Dieu m'y veuille tenir.*"

It was admired by one of the stenographers at her trial, who testified at her Rehabilitation Trial, which came in 1450, twenty years later, after France had been cleared of the English. He said that Joan had often complained that she was being asked too many subtle questions, and he gave this question as an example—and he added that those who were questioning her were amazed at her answer, and stopped, and did not ask her more.

The other is no less appreciative. Paul Doncoeur, who has edited the record of Joan's examination, suggests in a note that Joan's answer here is contained in a prayer which is part of the instructions of the Church. This makes Joan's answer perfect, as any lawyer will agree.

❊ 100 ❊

"When you swear, swear seriously and solemnly, but at the same time with a smile, for a smile is the twin sister of seriousness."

PLATO, WHO WROTE this in his Sixth Epistle, was as sophisticated as he was wise. I like to think, however, that this remark sprang simply from a proper attitude toward life and living.

The best illustration I can think of is Joan of Arc smiling when she signed her statement of abjuration, confessing that she had grievously sinned in falsely pretending to have had revelations from God through Saint Katherine and Saint Margaret, etc. Four days later she retracted, and then as a relapsed heretic she was burned to death on May 30, 1431.

The fact that she smiled is sufficiently attested by the testimony of several witnesses. Manchon, the chief notary, who had reported the testimony at

Joan's trial, was there and he testified that she smiled. Du Désert, who had been one of her judges, testified, "When she laughed as she pronounced certain words in the abjuration, an English doctor in theology said to the Bishop of Beauvais that he did ill to admit this abjuration and that it was a mockery, to which the Bishop told him he lied." Jean de Mailly, the Bishop of Noyon, who was there, testified that "after her abjuration many said that it was only a farce and that she made it only to mock at it, and that it seemed to him Joan herself scarcely cared and held it of no account." I take this testimony from Régine Pernoud's book on Joan's Rehabilitation Trial.

I see no reason to disbelieve this testimony, though, to be sure, testimony at hearings called for the purpose of rehabilitating Joan may very well have been under some pressure, and no doubt Joan's abjuration, like a plea of guilty, called for some explanation. There seems to be no evidence that she was hysterical. She had just rebuked the priest who had been preaching at her when he called her king, Charles the Seventh, a heretic. "*Ne parle pas de mon roi, il est bon chrestien.*" Joan had shown no signs of hysteria at her trial. On the contrary. One of her answers on cross-examination had been the best answer ever given to a prosecuting attorney. It may be that the fact she smiled was brought in to show that her abjuration was not sincere, and the English doctor of theology was right, Joan was making a farce of it and mocking her judges. I find this hard to take, but the fact she smiled remains none the less true. So it would appear to the English doctor and to many others of those present, but not to me. I think Joan smiled seriously and solemnly, as Plato said one should.

❉ 101 ❉

"I am your anointed Queen. I will never be by violence constrained to do anything. I thank God I am endued with such qualities that if I were turned out of the Realm in my petticoat, I were able to live in any place in Christendom."

AND SURELY there was a smile on Queen Elizabeth's lips when she told this to a Committee of both Houses of Parliament, and equally surely no one thought she was joking.

❉ 102 ❉

YOU DON'T need to smile. Usual behavior in unusual circumstances may serve the same purpose and carry the same attitude. Abraham Lincoln has given us the best example of this that I know.

On his way to Washington for his first inauguration, Lincoln stopped in New York. Walt Whitman was in the crowd in front of the Astor when Lincoln got out of the carriage.

"I shall not easily forget the first time I ever saw Abraham Lincoln. It must have been about the 18th or 19th of February, 1861. It was rather a pleasant afternoon, in New York City, as he arrived there from the West, to remain a few hours, and then pass on to Washington, to prepare for his inauguration. I saw him on Broadway, near the site of the present Post-office. He came down, I think from Canal Street, to stop at the Astor House. The broad spaces, sidewalks, and streets in the neighborhood, and for some distance, were crowded with solid masses of people, many thousands. The omnibuses and other vehicles had all been turn'd off, leaving an unusual hush in that busy part of the city. Presently two or three shabby hack barouches made their way with some difficulty through the crowd, and drew up at the Astor House entrance. A tall figure step'd out of the centre of these barouches, paus'd leisurely on the sidewalk, look'd up at the granite walls and looming architecture of the grand old hotel—then, after a relieving stretch of arms and legs, turn'd round for over a minute to slowly and good-humoredly scan the appearance of the vast and silent crowds. There were no speeches —no compliments—no welcome—as far as I could hear, not a word said. Still much anxiety was conceal'd in that quiet. Cautious persons had fear'd some mark'd insult or indignity to the President-elect—for he possess'd no personal popularity at all in New York City, and very little political. But it was evidently tacitly agreed that if the few political supporters of Mr. Lincoln present would entirely abstain from any demonstration on their side, the immense majority, who were anything but support-ers, would abstain on their side also. The result was a sulky, unbroken silence, such as certainly never before characterized so great a New York crowd.

"Almost in the same neighborhood I distinctly remember'd seeing Lafayette on his visit to Amer-ica in 1825. I had also personally seen and heard, various years afterward, how Andrew Jackson, Clay, Webster, Hungarian Kossuth, Filibuster Walker, the Prince of Wales on his visit, and other celebres, native and foreign, had been welcom'd there—all that indescribable human roar and magnetism, un-like any other sound in the universe—the glad exult-ing thunder-shouts of countless unloos'd throats of men! But on this occasion, not a voice—not a sound. From the top of an omnibus (driven up one side, close by, and block'd by the curbstone and the crowds), I had, I say, a capital view of it all, and especially of Mr. Lincoln, his look and gait—his perfect composure and coolness—his unusual and uncouth height, his dress of complete black, stove-pipe hat push'd back on the head, dark-brown com-plexion, seam'd and wrinkled yet canny-looking face, black, bushy head of hair, disproportionately long neck, and his hands held behind as he stood observing the people. He look'd with curiosity upon that immense sea of faces, and the sea of faces return'd the look with similar curiosity. In both there was a dash of comedy, almost farce, such as Shakespear puts in his blackest tragedies. The crowd that hemm'd around consisted I should think of thirty to forty thousand men, not a single one his personal friend—while I have no doubt (so frenzied were the ferments of the time) many an assassin's knife and pistol lurk'd in hip or breast-pocket there, ready, soon as break and riot came.

"But no break or riot came. The tall figure gave another relieving stretch or two of arms and legs; then with moderate pace, and accompanied by a few unknown looking persons, ascended the portico-steps of the Astor House, disappear'd through its broad entrance—and the dumb-show ended."

❋ 103 ❋

"There never was a merry world since the fairies left off dancing, and the parson left conjuring."

So John Selden remarked in his *Table Talk*, somewhere along the beginning of the seventeenth century.

"Well, I say, it was never merry world in England since gentlemen came up."

This is Shakespear about the same time.

NEARLY THREE centuries later, in 1884, the matter was brought to the attention of the Home Secretary, who was then Sir William Harcourt. He met a delegation and replied as follows:

> "HOME OFFICE
> March 22, 1884.

"I am obliged by your letter.

"What I said to the deputation requesting me to put down itinerant shows, though spoken on the spur of the moment, expresses a very strong conviction in my mind.

"We are doing what we can for the improvement

of the houses and homes of the poor, for their health and their education. We have already done a good deal in securing for them greater abundance of cheap food and other things which are the necessaries of existence. All this is good in itself, but it is by no means the whole or even the best part of life.

"What is to be desired is not only that people should live, but that they should enjoy life, and by enjoyment of life I do not mean mere physical comfort. No doubt it is more difficult though it is by no means impossible to be cheery when you are uncomfortable. But people who have every comfort in life are often the most dull and discontented.

"A small minority of the world perhaps devote themselves too much to pleasure, but the greater part of mankind—at least of English kind—have far too little pleasure in life. A good many people deliberately choose to be dull. They seem to think that there is something respectable and even virtuous in a decorous solemnity of existence. To my mind there is nothing so doleful as the class of people who seem to consider that the whole duty of man is summed up in going about in a tall hat and a black coat with an establishment to match. There is nothing so ineffably depressing as the joyless monotony of the well-to-do classes. I don't believe they are a bit better for it, and I am sure they are a good deal less happy than they might be. But that is their affair, and in a free country people must be allowed to be as dreary and morose as they please. But don't

213

let us inflict our dreariness as if it were a good thing on others who are willing to be merry and have too little opportunity of being so.

"After all joy is the greatest of all blessings and we should welcome it, however it comes. The great mass of the people of this country have far too little amusement, not because they don't want it but because they can't get it. We cannot organize fun as we do education and drainage—I wish we could; but all attempts at regulating jollity are a mistake and a failure. The merit of the 'itinerant showman' is that it is *his* interest to find out and to know what his public patrons want, and to cater for them in the way that pleases them most and which they can afford. I like their 'shows.' I think I have seen as many of them as most people myself and helped a good many to see them. The 'patter' of the show-man is one of the most interesting and delightful specimens of indigenous wit and vernacular eloquence which remains to us—far more interesting and quite as instructive as a good many of the solemn performances to which it is my fate to listen. I enjoy the humours and bustle of a fair with its merry-go-rounds and its cockshies, its fortune-tellers, cheap jacks, Merry Andrews, its acrobats, its theatres, and the shouts of the children, more musical than any concert. I used to like it principally for my own sake—now I like it more for the sake of others.

"The best social reformer is the man who realizes most the best thing you can do for people is to make them *jolly*. This spirit of delight is like the sun which illuminates the picture and glorifies the landscape. Let us have all we can of it and especially let us get it for the young whom nature intended to be gay. As years advance we can only hope to see it reflected from the hearts of others. In London how difficult is this to procure. In this wilderness of counting-houses and shops and comfortable dwellings and dilapidated lodgings there is room, it is true, for theatres and concert rooms ever multiplying for the rich, but where are the playing-fields of the poor? I rejoice when I see an accidental space occupied by the yellow caravan or the booth of the showman which offers a precarious entertainment to those who find too little joy between the gutter and the grave.

"I certainly by no act of mine will snatch away their lucky windfalls of fun. I should as soon think of putting down Punch at the corner of the streets. I hope that we shall not turn up our respectable noses at the rude and simple pleasures of the poor, and even if we do not understand them ourselves or even suffer some small inconvenience from them, be glad that they give a momentary mirth to those whose lives are sadder than our own."

❋ 104 ❋

". . . but man, proud man
Dressed in a little brief authority,
Most ignorant of what he's most assured,
His glassy essence, like an angry ape,
Plays such fantastic tricks before high heaven
As make the angels weep; who, with our spleens,
Would all themselves laugh mortal."

THIS IS Isabella in *Measure for Measure*, and I
want to make it clear, to begin with, that to
Shakespear in his time and in the Globe, this word
spleen meant more than it now means to us. It re-
veals an important difference between us and the
Elizabethans. For we have taken all the merriment
out of the word. To them, the spleen was the seat
of all the emotions, hilarity and laughter as well as
the melancholy or ill temper you will find in the
dictionaries of today; all our passions, not just our
spites and angers. Passion to the Elizabethans was
admirable as well as evil. It was any large and swift
emotion, like lightning "that in a spleen unfolds
both heaven and earth," as Lysander told Hermia
in *A Midsummer Night's Dream*.

About angels, it seems that angels, at any rate our angels, are unable to laugh. Men laugh. Neither beasts nor angels can. I may say we once had a poodle who smiled. I am sure of that, but I think she smiled out of embarrassment and self-consciousness. Perhaps angels can't even do that. At any rate, I don't think they can smile, far less laugh. When Abdiel, the guardian angel of Maurice de'Esparvieu, first appeared, and Madame de Aubels most unexpectedly caught sight of him, standing between the mantelpiece and the wardrobe, at a ludicrously inopportune moment, even for a guardian angel, Abdiel was as solemn as any of the Church Fathers he started to quote from. And yet Abdiel was an angel in revolt, as Anatole France tells us.

Beatrice, Dante's Beatrice, remains human enough to smile, but I don't think she ever laughs. I cannot think of any even semi-divine person who laughs, except the Gods on Olympus. They "laugh mortal." They all laughed unquenchably in the first book of the *Iliad* when Hephaistos stumbled passing the wine. All the Gods laughed when Aphrodite was caught in the net with Ares. Only the Goddesses were too modest to come and look.

It strikes me as a pity that our Gods are too dignified to laugh.

"The total absence of humour from the Bible," Whitehead remarked to Lucien Price, "is one of the most singular things in all literature." "Goethe notices it," Lucien said, "in the Prologue to *Faust*. Mephistopheles is made to twit God with his lack

217

of humour: 'My pathos would but move your Grace to laughter, had you not long since laughter quite abjured.' "

I cannot recall any picture of Jesus smiling. He wept, but I don't think he ever smiled. The Virgin Mary smiles in some of her pictures, and I wonder if this may not be one reason why she is so much adored. And, of course, Santa Claus is jolly. I think we'd have done better if the Irish had had more to do with our religious traditions. Yeats, in his "Cradle Song," has the wonderful line, "God's laughing in Heaven, To see you so good." And I have no doubt that the northern gods, the gods of the Eddas, laughed as loud as men.

✲ 105 ✲

But there is a scene in the Babylonian Talmud
where Jehovah showed he could laugh like an Olym-
pian. Here it is, in the version that Edmond Cahn
put into his book, *The Moral Decision.*

Rabbi Eliezer is engaged in an argument with his
colleagues over a technical point in the interpreta-
tion of the law:

"After exhausting all his resources of precedent,
distinction, analogy, and citation of textual authority without convincing any of them, Rabbi Eliezer
becomes desperate and cries out, 'If the law agrees
with me, let this tree prove it!' Thereupon the tree
leaps a hundred cubits from its place, some say four
hundred cubits. But the other judges calmly retort,
'No proof can be adduced from a tree.' Then he
says, 'If the law agrees with me, let this stream of
water prove it!' At this the stream of water flows
backwards. The others rejoin however, 'No proof
can be adduced from a stream of water.' Again he
calls out, 'If the law agrees with me, let the walls of
the house prove it!' Whereupon the walls begin to
fall, but Rabbi Joshua, one of the sages present,
rebukes them, saying, 'When scholars are engaged
in a legal dispute, what right have you to interfere?'

219

And so they do not fall, out of respect for Rabbi Joshua, nor do they resume the upright, out of respect for Rabbi Eliezer, but remain standing and inclined. Finally Rabbi Eliezer says, 'If the law agrees with me, let it be proved from heaven!' At that moment a Heavenly Voice cries out, 'Why do you dispute with Rabbi Eliezer, seeing that in all matters the law agrees with him?' For a space the assembly sits transfixed, but almost immediately Rabbi Joshua rises from his seat and exclaims, 'The law is not in heaven! It was given on Mount Sinai. We pay no attention to a Heavenly Voice.'

"Soon thereafter one of the Rabbis happens to meet the prophet Elijah, who, having been alive when he was transported into the celestial regions, remains able to converse with mortals. The prophet is asked, 'What did the Holy One, blessed be He, do at that point?' Elijah replies, 'He laughed with joy, saying, "My sons have defeated Me, My sons have defeated Me." ' "

MAY IT NOT be a sign of superior power to be able to laugh as well as weep? There are many occasions when it is hard to say which is more appropriate; and how many there are that call for both! The deepest grief can run full circle, as every clown of us knows.

Or let us call ourselves jesters rather than clowns. Then we shall be with Niels Bohr, for he said this about our problem: "In the balance between seriousness and humor characteristic of all great works of art, we are reminded of complementary aspects conspicuous of children's play and no less appreciated in mature life. Indeed, if we endeavoured always to speak quite seriously, we would run the risk of appearing very soon ridiculously tedious to our listeners and ourselves. But if we try to joke all the time, we rapidly bring ourselves and our listeners too—if the witticisms have point—to the desperate mood which Shakespeare with such genius has pictured for us in the role of the jesters in his immortal dramas."

Both seriousness and humor, laughter as well as gravity. Both are necessary to great works of art. Both are equally necessary to mankind. If a man only jokes, I agree with Bohr that he is desperate. But if a man is never anything but serious, he's worse than tedious. He thinks he's God, and not a very good god at that.

❀ 106 ❀

"... a crazy act, in which our felicities and our filth are lodged pell-mell together; and our supreme delight has something faint and plaintive about it, like pain. I think what Plato says is so, that the Gods made mankind for fun and to be their toy.

" 'But why, then, such a savage joke?' "

A VAST and nasty joke? Montaigne thought it was. The loveliest of our faculties coupled to the grossest of our necessities.

Or are we only imagining that the Gods are making fun of us and laughing at us? May not delights be the proper companions of necessities?

❀ 107 ❀

"A time to weep."

W HY IT IS regarded as unmanly to weep, I do not see at all. It is no more unmanly than it is sentimental; and a good man is something less than a whole man if he is not sentimental. Angels can weep, but not laugh. Men can do both. Tom Jones bursts into tears repeatedly. The toughest hero of them all, Odysseus, weeps. The tears ran down his cheeks when he heard Demodocus, the minstrel, sing of Troy, and he pulled his mantle across his face, and when Demodocus sang again, Odysseus again wept. Then Alcinoös noticed it and thought it was time to get up from the luncheon and start the sports.

Odysseus was sitting with the tears streaming down his face, on the headland on Calypso's island, looking toward Ithaca, when Hermes came to tell her that Odysseus was to go home.

❈ 108 ❈

Whitehead, in his Adventures of Ideas, *speaks of Plato's final conviction, toward the end of his life, "that the divine element in the world is to be conceived as a persuasive agency and not as a coercive agency."*

THIS DOCTRINE," Whitehead goes on to say, "should be looked upon as one of the greatest intellectual discoveries in the history of religion."

And the only solution of the dilemma of an Almighty God, or any god that is omnipotent as well as omniscient, what with all the cruelty, misery, and evil chance so obvious in the world. What are we to think of an Almighty and Omnipotent God that permits such things? "As flies to wanton boys, are we to the gods. They kill us for their sport." Absolute power corrupts absolutely. *Corruptio optimi pessima.*

So it would seem, not only according to our human standards of behavior, but, as it would seem, according to His own divine precepts. For among us there have been, and there are now, men and women who within their small and mortal powers are better by His own standards than any Omnipotent God that permits such things to happen.

It was a grim remark that Jesus made, according to John. There was a man who had been blind from birth, and they asked Jesus, "Master, who did sin, this man or his parents, that he was born blind?" Jesus answered, "Neither hath this man sinned, nor his parents: but that the works of God should be manifest in him."

If the works of God are intelligible to man, if good and evil are what we think they are, a god who is both omnipotent and benevolent is a contradiction. Humanly speaking, good and evil are antithetical. They are opposites. Each is the contrary, or subcontrary to be precise, of the other. Neither can logically—and that is humanly—exist without the other. Move the zero point, which is the point be-

224

tween good and evil where you cannot quite say whether something is either good or evil. If you move it to the left, there is more good than evil in the world, humanly measured. Move it to the right, and there is more evil than good. Not unless you move it all the way across, to the edge of this world, or beyond, can this world be either wholly good and under the governance of a Being both omnipotent and benevolent, or wholly evil and the work of a devil.

"Evil can never be done away with, Theodorus. For the good must always have its contrary. Nor can evil have any place among the gods. So it prowls about here below among us humans."

There appear to be three alternatives. God may not be wholly benevolent. If He is not, He is not worth our worship. We can find a number of men and women better worth worshiping. Or God may not be omniscient. But if He is not, how can we be sure He is wiser than some of our own wise men?

The third alternative is Plato's final conviction, that God was not coercive, but only persuasive. And is this not Christianity? Whitehead went on to say:

"The essence of Christianity is the appeal to the life of Christ as a revelation of the nature of God and of his agency in the world. The record is fragmentary, inconsistent, and uncertain. It is not necessary for me to express any opinion as to the proper reconstruction of the most likely tale of historic fact. Such a procedure would be useless, without value, and entirely out of place in this book. But there can be no doubt as to what elements in the record have evoked a response from all that is best in human nature. The Mother, the Child, and the bare manger: the lowly man, homeless and self-forgetful, with his message of peace, love, and sympathy: the suffering, the agony, the tender words as life ebbed, the final despair: and the whole with the authority of supreme victory.

"I need not elaborate. Can there be any doubt that the power of Christianity lies in its revelation in act, of that which Plato divined in theory?"

The trouble is, too many of our creeds and theologies are not only monotheistic but monopolistic. If God is not a coercive agency, someone or something else may be; and this they dare not concede. A merely persuasive agency might not succeed, even in the long run. More than persuasion may be needed against the competition of evil.

Consider the power of persuasion from our point of view, and you will see its shortcomings as a method of control. B. F. Skinner said:

"The methods of education, moral discourse, and persuasion are acceptable not because they recognize the freedom of the individual or his right to dissent, but because they make only *partial* contributions to the control of his behavior. The freedom they recognize is freedom from a more coercive form of control. The dissent which they tolerate is the possible effect of other determiners of action. Since these sanctioned methods are frequently ineffective, we have been able to convince ourselves that they do not represent control at all. When they show too much strength to permit disguise, we give them other names and suppress them as energetically as we suppress the use of force. Education grown too powerful is rejected as propaganda or 'brain-washing,' while really effective persuasion is decried as 'undue influence,' 'demagoguery,' 'seduction,' and so on."

I should myself deny even the power of persuasion, let alone coercion, to whatever divine element there may be in the world. The most credible and adorable deity would be one without power, needing none and relying solely on the ancient paradox of the power of love. But no theological monopolist is going to drop the notion of an Almighty God just to get his closed fist out of the narrow neck of a dilemma.

❊ 109 ❊

"Her privates, we."

I AM SURE Justice Holmes would have smiled at my bawdy caption, even though, or rather because, what I am going to quote from him goes to the very heart of Holmes's faith. For he would agree with Montaigne when he said, "Those who refuse to express serious opinions playfully, someone said, act like one who fears to worship a saint's image unless it wears a fig leaf."

Holmes asked, "What kind of a world do you want?" and added, "We will not dispute about tastes. The man of the future may want something different." Then Holmes went on and here, I think, stated his faith:

"But who of us could endure a world, although cut up into five-acre lots and having no man upon it who was not well fed and well housed, without the divine folly of honor, without the senseless passion for knowledge outreaching the flaming bounds of the possible, without ideals the essence of which is that they never can be achieved?"

I break in to remind you of the rest of this Lucretian quotation, as Bailey translated it: "And so it was that the lively force of his mind won its way, and he passed on far beyond the fiery walls of the world, and in mind and spirit traversed the boundless whole." The Latin is no better:

> Ergo vivida vis animi pervicit, et extra
> Processit longe flammantia moenia mundi
> Atque omne immensum peragravit, mente
> animoque.

Holmes knew what he was quoting, but he had no thought that his mind could go beyond the flaming bounds. This was a "senseless passion," he wrote Laski: "I see not the slightest reason for believing that our reason and our truth are cosmic ultimates or anything more than our own *flammantia moenia*."

Holmes goes on:

"I do not know what is true. I do not know the meaning of the universe. But in the midst of doubt, in the collapse of creeds, there is one thing I do not doubt, that no man who lives in the same world with most of us can doubt, and that is that the faith is true and adorable which leads a soldier to throw away his life in obedience to a blindly accepted duty, in a cause which he little understands, in a plan of campaign of which he has no notion, under tactics of which he does not see the use."

Holmes said this in 1895. Twenty-odd years later, in 1918, he said no less, even a bit more:

"That the universe has in it more than we understand, that the private soldiers have not been told the plan of campaign, or even that there is one, rather than some vaster unthinkable to which every predicate is an impertinence, has no bearing upon our conduct. We still shall fight—all of us because we want to live, some, at least, because we want to realize our spontaneity and prove our powers, for the joy of it, and we may leave to the unknown the supposed final valuation of that which in any event has value to us. It is enough for us that the universe has produced us and has within it, as less than it, all that we believe and love. If we think of our existence not as that of a little god outside, but as that of a ganglion within, we have the infinite behind us. It gives us our only but our adequate significance."

"Life is peculiar," said Jeremy. "As compared with what?" asked the Spider. I don't know where this colloquy comes from. Nor does my wife, who gave it to Ferris Greenslet and me, and we put it into our *Practical Cogitator*. We had inquiries. The Fountain Valley School wrote Ferris that its librarian had searched all of Hugh Walpole's Jeremy books and failed to find it. This must be another Jeremy, but the Spider is a disciple of Holmes.

It would be a cynic or a bigot who called this soldier's faith less than devotion. Holmes has been called a skeptic, an agnostic, an atheist, as no doubt he was; and, from a number of points of view, a heretic. On a number of subjects he was an agnostic, and on many more a skeptic, and about God an atheist. But only a cynic or a bigot would say that Holmes lacked faith. He had an admiration which amounted to reverence for a man's devotion to a cause he could little understand, which he could not even be sure existed.

It was a soldier's faith, but war and battle are not the only things that raise questions which are inscrutably impossible to understand. Holmes believed many things were impossible to understand, and his reverence embraced every purpose that a man could not understand and yet was willing to serve. I think that Holmes admired an admitted ignorance of the ends as much as he admired proficiency in the means.

> "And pardner, tell my friends below,
> I took a raging dream in tow;
> And if I never laid it low,
> I never turned it loose."

TO GO ON FROM HERE:

LET ME *say, to begin with, that you will find a good deal here from* The Practical Cogitator, *the anthology that Ferris Greenslet and I put together and Houghton, Mifflin published first in 1945. For I have been as little able to keep out of that anthology as a great many others. Indeed I was not always aware of where I was until I looked up. I am grateful to Ferris Greenslet and to Houghton, Mifflin, and anyone who is at all familiar with the* Cogitator *will see why.*

1. This is from the Apocrypha, II Esdras, chapter 14, verse 25.

It was one of these candles that Latimer lit on October 16, 1555, in Oxford when he and Ridley were burned at the stake for their Protestant heresies. "Be of good comfort, Master Ridley," Hugh Latimer said, "and play the man. We shall this day light such a candle by God's grace in England as I trust shall never be put out."

2. This is 64 of Pascal's *Pensées,* in Brunschvicg's edition. There is an English translation in the Everyman Library, with an introduction by T. S. Eliot. Pascal was obsessed by Montaigne, at once seduced and revolted; and Pascal confessed as much to Monsieur de Saci. Their short interview is—well, it's on a par

with Gorki's account of his conversations with Tolstoi. George Pearce translated it in his *Miscellaneous Writings of Pascal*.

T. S. Eliot, in his introduction to the *Pensées* in the Everyman Edition, says that "Pascal studied Montaigne with the intention of demolishing him. Yet, in the *Pensées*, at the very end of his life, we find passage after passage, and the slighter they are the more significant, almost 'lifted' out of Montaigne, down to a figure of speech or a word. . . . Indeed, by the time a man knew Montaigne well enough to attack him, he would already be thoroughly infected by him."

Eliot goes on, "It would, however, be grossly unfair to Pascal, to Montaigne, and indeed to French literature, to leave the matter at that." If Montaigne, Eliot says, "had been no more than Voltaire, he could not have affected Pascal at all. . . . What makes Montaigne a very great figure is that he succeeded, God knows how —for Montaigne very likely did not know that he had done it—it is not the sort of thing that men *can* observe about themselves, for it is essentially bigger than the individual's consciousness—he succeeded in giving expression to the skepticism of *every* human being."

I said that Pascal was *obsessed* by Montaigne. Eliot says he was *infected* by him.

The Virginia Woolf is in *The Common Reader*, on page 32 of the Harcourt, Brace Harvest edition. "Just on the far side of language," but only just, only a little beyond our reach, not too far to try to reach. Everyone has their own best examples. I find that what I like best of Yeats is, I think, just beyond my fingertips. So too is the little I have read of Rilke. Anyway, we'd rather reach for a meaning than have it passed to us.

The DeQuincey is in his *Letters to a Young Man*.

The Coleridge comes near the end of chapter 14 of his *Biographia Literaria*; but I was satisfied by I. A. Richards' book, *Coleridge on the Imagination*, 1934.

The sentence from Coleridge's *Note-books* was quoted by Humphrey House in his Clark Lectures for 1951–2, published by Hart-Davis. I found it there on page 150.

The first book to read on this subject seems to me to be any book of verse, the one nearest to your hand; any one where the meaning is not quite obvious. If you will compare what a poem means to you with what you think it meant to the author, I think you will prefer your own version, just as he may prefer his, or your friend, hers.

3. There are two good ways to start reading Edmund Wilson. One is to begin with the first thing of his you come across, whatever it may be, his little book on *The Scrolls from the Dead Sea*, which first came out in *The New Yorker*, or his book of short stories, *Memoirs of Hecate County*, which was banned in New York and in Los Angeles, or his critical studies, of which *The Triple Thinkers* is one. The other way is to get a volume of his book reviews, *Classics and Commercials*, or *A Literary Chronicle, 1920–1950*. If you do this, start with what he wrote on what you are least interested in. For Wilson is both an interpreter and an instigator. I did this with the collection called *A Literary Chronicle* with great success. I read the piece on Kafka, and now I know I never need read him; his piece on Sartre, and my interest was quickened; his piece on Faulkner and the Civil Rights Program, and my understanding

234

was bettered. If there is anything that Wilson can't make you as interested in as he is himself, you are either an intellectual or an emotional specialist.

4. To what editor or publisher do we owe more than to John Heminge and Henry Condell? They were the two friends of Shakespear who gathered up the prompt copies and his manuscripts and got out the plays in their first folio edition. And has any library a more miserly hoard of books than the Folger Library's seventy-seven—or is it seventy-nine?—copies? If you are in Washington, go in and ask to see them. They used to be kept in the safe. Gape, but don't touch.

In their preface, Heminge and Condell say, "Read him, therefore; and again, and again: And if you do not like him, surely you are in some manifest danger, not to understand him."

5. Don't try to find this in Edith Wharton. You will find the Aristotle in his *Poetics*, 1460A; and Toynbee's translation in his volume V on page 614.

6. *Tom Jones* by Henry Fielding, book 16, chapter 5.

You will remember the way Bottom took such pains not to scare the ladies. It is at the beginning of the third act of A *Midsummer Night's Dream.*

For the Coleridge, go to the same chapter 14 of the *Biographia Literaria.* The Richards is in his *Practical Criticism*, Harcourt, Brace, page 277, which is one of those splendid books that you should read some of, but need not read all of.

7. Mr. Justice Darling was a British judge, who published a number of his remarks under the happy title

of *Scintillae Juris* in 1877. Stevens and Haynes, of Temple Bar, republished them in 1914.

8. I don't suppose it is possible to read the Maxims of the Duke de La Rochefoucauld—there are more than five hundred—any more than it is possible to wear a handful, two handfuls, of unset precious stones. You can pick the Duke's Maxims up one by one and admire them, but if you do this very often you will find that they are all of the same stone, cut differently and reflecting different lights, but all of a kind. For they all, almost all, presuppose the tenable but oversimple and uninteresting theory that all human motives spring from only one thing, self-love, self-esteem, *amour propre*. Too simple, I say; for it ignores all human contradictions. How different are the *Pensées* of Pascal, his contemporary in the France of Louis XIV, and indeed in the same society, except when La Rochefoucauld was at the wars or Pascal absorbed in religion! Pascal's *Pensées* are not precious stones, they are pieces and snatches of living tissue.

9. Richard Whately, fellow of Oriel College, Oxford, author of a popular book on logic, and another on rhetoric; and from 1831 to his death in 1863 the Protestant Archbishop of Dublin. To the Evangelicals, it was said, he was no better than a latitudinarian. He wrote a satire, *Historic Doubts Relative to Napoleon Buonoparte*. I don't know where you'll find more of his Apophthegms than the four, of which this is one, in the Oxford Dictionary of Quotations. One of the others is "Happiness is no laughing matter."

For the Autolycus, *The Winter's* Tale, act 4, scene 4.

236

Stimson's memorandum to President Roosevelt is in McGeorge Bundy's book, *On Active Service;* Harper's, 1947, 1948, II, 644.

10. Sir Frederick Pollock to Justice Holmes, July 2, 1928; in volume II page 225 of the *Holmes-Pollock Letters,* edited by Mark Howe.

If you want to be cynical, ponder Paul Valéry's crack, "The truth is a means. It is not the only one."

11. Justice Holmes to Harold J. Laski, October 12, 1919; in volume I page 214 of the *Holmes-Laski Letters,* equally well edited by Mark Howe.

12. *Pudd'nhead Wilson* is a good book for a young lawyer starting practice in a new community. *The Just and the Unjust,* by James Gould Cozzens, is a better one, wherever he starts.

I have done far less than justice, to say nothing of understanding, when I speak of *Pudd'nhead Wilson* as a book for lawyers. Read F. R. Leavis' introduction to the Grove Press Edition, 1955.

13. Nicholas Bacon was an attorney in London in the sixteenth century. In 1553 he gave an adverse opinion of law to his friend Matthew Parker, then Dean of Lincoln, later the Archbishop of Canterbury, and Bacon added these sentences as a postscript. His youngest son was Francis Bacon, a great philosopher, a great lawyer, and what's more, a man that many have thought capable of writing Shakespear's plays. Is there a higher compliment?

14. I am not a Trollope lover. I read *Orley Farm* for the sake of its law and its lawyers. Let me add it to my list of novels for lawyers.

15. I don't think this is in Boswell. I found it referred to in *Johnsonian Miscellanies,* edited by G. B. Hill, volume I, page 327, note.

16. Henry Cecil, I understand, is the pseudonym of a British barrister who writes excellent novels. *Brothers in Law* is as good reading for a lawyer as Cozzens' *The Just and the Unjust.* This from *Friends at Court.*

Edmund M. Morgan is a professor of law at Vanderbilt University. The first quotation is on page 11 of his book, *Basic Problems of Evidence,* which he wrote for the American Law Institute's Committee on Continuing Legal Education in 1954. Write to the Director, John E. Mulder, 133 South 36th Street, Philadelphia, Pennsylvania. Morgan's Carpentier Lectures were published by the Columbia University Press in 1956; page 128.

17. The Darwin is in *More Letters of Charles Darwin,* edited by Francis Darwin, London, 1903, volume I, page 195.

Lucien Price's *Dialogues of Alfred North Whitehead,* page 278, Atlantic Monthly Press, 1954. If you will read these *Dialogues* first, I suggest you then read the first six chapters of Whitehead's *Science and the Modern World,* and go as far into each of the later chapters as you can understand. I find I can get through several paragraphs. Then I take a running start, and get a little further. After you have got as far as you can,

238

read that very great book, Whitehead's *Adventures of Ideas*.

18. This is Percy W. Bridgman in his *Reflections of a Physicist*, Philosophical Library, 1950, pages 369–70. There is a second enlarged edition. Unless you already know his operational thinking, you'd better read the opening chapters of his book, *The Logic of Modern Physics*, Macmillan, 1927; or the passages from it in *The Practical Cogitator*, pages 43–45.

19. Hobbes, in the *Leviathan*, in chapter 6.
The Pascal is *Pensées* 18.
The Schrödinger is in his *Nature and the Greeks*, Cambridge University Press, 1954, page 6.
I. A. Richards heard Oppenheimer make this remark about science, and Richards asks, "How otherwise could it advance?"; see his last book, *Speculative Instruments*, Routledge and Kegan Paul, 1955, page 174.

21. The stenographer's version is a little different, and so far as I am concerned, less accurate. You will find it in Irving Dilliard's collection of Hand, *The Spirit of Liberty*, which Alfred A. Knopf published in 1952 and again, later, enlarged. It reads: "You remember in *The Cloister and the Hearth*, in tight moments how Gerard's companion used to say: '*Courage, mon ami, le diable est mort!* No, my friends, the devil isn't dead; but take heart of grace; we shall get him yet!"

22. The four lines about Harry Percy, *Henry IV, Part Two*, act 1, scene 2. The two lines on Time, from *Troilus and Cressida*, act 3, scene 3.
I took the phrase, "snatch a grace beyond the reach

of art," from William Hazlitt's *Characteristics* 139. He put it in quotes, but he does not say from whom he took them. I don't see that it matters.

The earliest known version of *Tom o'Bedlam* is 1615.

23. By an anonymous poet, quoted in Chamber's Encyclopedia from Prince's *Worthies of Devon*.

24. *Lear*, act 5, scene 2.
Love's Labor's Lost, act 4, scene 2.
Twelfth Night, act 1, scene 2.
The first Goethe is in Biedermann's *Ausgewählte Gespräche*, page 526; the second in Eckermann, September 18, 1823. Didn't Rilke say somewhere that Eckermann had written the greatest of German books? I am grateful to Hans Zinsser for telling me to read it.

To go on about ripeness, there is a paragraph in Thoreau's *Journal* that almost persuades me there is some foundation for Eliot's emotion. It is this: "There is no ripeness which is not, so to speak, something ultimate in itself, and not merely a perfected means to a higher end. In order to be ripe it must serve a transcendent use. The ripeness of a leaf, being perfected, leaves the tree and never returns to it. It has nothing to do with any other fruit which the tree may bear, and only the genius of the poet can pluck it. The fruit of a tree is neither in the seed nor the timber, the full-grown tree, but it is simply the highest use to which it can be put." March 7, 1859. You will find it almost accurately reprinted in that selection from the *Journal*, called *Early Spring in Massachusetts*, published by Houghton, Mifflin. Buy this when you see it, and also its three companions, *Summer*, *Autumn*, and *Winter*.

25. Emerson's *Journal*, May 24, 1847.

27. My Oxford Dictionary of Quotations tells me that this is in Chaucer's *Parliament of Fowls*, which I've neither read nor mean to. The Lord Chief Justice Coke, in his *Four Institutes*, embodied the law of England, better even than the Lord Chancellor in Gilbert and Sullivan's *Iolanthe*, down very nearly, all too nearly, to Blackstone's famous *Commentaries* in 1776.

In Milton's *Iconoclastes*, chapter 23.

28. I took this from Dominique Aury's review of the Hansons' life of Toulouse-Lautrec in *The New York Times* Book Review section, June 17, 1956.

You could follow up these thoughts by taking Shakespear's sonnets as an example. Two poets draw the issue. Wordsworth, praising the sonnet, claimed, ". . . with this key Shakespear unlocked his heart." Browning, writing a poem which he called "House," in defense of a poet's right of privacy, laughed at Wordsworth.

"Shall I sonnet-sing you about myself?
 Do I live in a house you would like to see?
 Is it scant of gear, has it store of pelf?
 'Unlock my heart with a sonnet-key'?"

And Browning ended the poem,

" 'Hoity-toity! A street to explore,
 Your house the exception! "With this same key
 Shakespeare unlocked his heart" once more!'
 Did Shakespeare? If so, the less Shakespeare he!"

This is also the opinion of John Jay Chapman. If you have, or can get, his little book, A *Glance Toward Shakespeare*, by all means read the chapter on "The Sonnets." Chapman takes the position that the Sonnets were works of art, not of passion; they were *literary* performances. He doubts whether anything has ever been said that explains them better than when Francis Meres referred to them as Shakespear's "sugared sonnets among his private friends." Yes, but this was in 1598; and we don't know how many or which of the sonnets we have Meres had read in 1598. They were not published until 1609, ten or more years later. Not all of them are "sugared"; and a few are savage.

Chapman is as candid a critic as there ever was. He goes on, "In those I have quoted thus far the element of paradox and *jeu d'esprit* is apparent; but when you come to the very great sonnets, where the poetic part is perfectly expressed and the idea is obvious, and represents a universal experience, it is almost impossible, while reading one of them, to keep one's head. We could almost swear that the poet is in love." He cites 98, 76, and 52. I find it utterly impossible to keep my head with 87, 90, 116, and 129. Try and see if *you* can keep *your* head.

The point Chapman makes is "that it is because Shakespeare's best sonnets are completely intellectual and dispassionate, that they make so personal an appeal. . . . Our own most inner chords can be made to vibrate, whether through music, architecture, or poetry, only by forces which have passed through some prism or crystal of the mind, and which are as impersonal as geometry."

And so we may ask—Should not the poet be the

pure craftsman, wholly the artist, and never himself? Should not all the passion be provided by the reader?

30. Boswell, volume 3, page 226, note 4.

Brookes's address to the Mathematical Association was reported in the London *Times*, April 7, 1956.

I owe the thought in my last paragraph to W. W. Sawyer, in his *Mathematician's Delight*; Pelican, 1943, page 34.

31. *As You Like It*, act 3, scene 2.

The Quine is from his *Methods of Logic*, Henry Holt and Company, 1950, page 200. Willard V. Quine is a professor of philosophy at Harvard. A couple of years ago, in 1953–54, he was the George Eastman professor at Oxford. He is now at the Institute for Advanced Study at Princeton for a year. A logical positivist, his writings are spangled with symbols, which makes them hard reading for me. In his latest book, *From a Logical Point of View*, Harvard University Press, 1953, he has suggested to me that a layman might read pages 1–27, 37–79, 102–107, 127–144; and Quine added, "If he feels abandoned in mid-air at page 144, he might use 156–159 for a landing."

I don't quite know what to recommend to go on from 31. There is, of course, C. K. Ogden's and I. A. Richards' *The Meaning of Meaning*, which I have read at and in and about, but never the whole of it. There is A. J. Ayer's *Language, Truth, and Logic*, published by Victor Gollancz. There is all that Whorf wrote, whom I quoted in 90; and see the note for the reference. There are the first few chapters of Bridgman's *The Logic of Modern Physics*, for which see the note to 18. I recommend Quine's next book, sight unseen, if it goes into the question of meaning.

I can't help citing myself. I tried to explain some of this business of meaning, not all of it, God knows, in my essay in *Jurisprudence in Action*, which Ralph M. Carson, for the Committee on Post-Admission Legal Education, got together and published for the Association of the Bar of the City of New York, Baker Voorhis & Co., 1953. And I tried again in my book *It's Your Law*, Harvard University Press, 1954, pages 44–81.

There is Michael Polanyi's Riddell Memorial Lecture, which was published by the Oxford University Press in 1946 under the title, *Science, Faith, and Society*. It is so hard to come by that I am going to offer you three paragraphs:

"The realms of science, of law, and of Protestant religion which I have taken as examples of modern cultural communities are each subject to control by their own body of opinion. Scientific opinion, legal theory, Protestant theology are all formed by the consensus of independent individuals, rooted in a common tradition. In law and in religion, it is true, there prevails a measure of official doctrinal compulsion from a centre, which is almost entirely absent from science. The difference is marked; yet in spite of such compulsion as legal and religious life are subjected to, the conscience of the judge and of the minister bears an important responsibility in acting as its own interpreter of the law or of the Christian faith. Thus the life of science, the law, and the Protestant Church all three stand in contrast to the constitution, say, of the Catholic Church which denies to the believer's conscience

244

the right to interpret the Christian dogma and reserves the final decision in such matters to his confessor. There is here the profound difference between two types of authority; one laying down general presuppositions, the other imposing *conclusions*. We may call the first a General, the latter a Specific Authority. . . .

"The main contrast between a regime of General Authority such as prevails in science, the law, etc., and the rule of a Specific Authority as constituted by the Catholic Church lies in the fact that the former leaves the decisions for interpreting traditional rules in the hands of numerous independent individuals while the latter centralizes such decisions at headquarters. A General Authority relies for the initiative in the gradual transformation of tradition on the intuitive impulses of the individual adherents of the community and it relies on their consciences to control their intuitions. The General Authority itself is but a more or less organized expression of the general opinion—scientific, legal, or religious—formed by the merging and interplay of all these individual contributions. Such a regime assumes that individual members are capable of making genuine contact with the reality underlying the existing tradition and of adding new and authentic interpretations to it. Innovation in this case is done at numerous growing points dispersed through the community, each of which may take the lead over the whole at any particular moment.

"A Specific Authority on the other hand makes all important reinterpretations and innovations by pronouncements from the centre. This centre alone is thought to have authentic contacts with the fundamental sources from which the existing tradition springs and can be renewed. Specific Authority demands therefore not only devotion to the tenets of a tradition but subordination of everyone's ultimate judgment to discretionary decision by an official centre."

33. More from the *Dialogues of Whitehead* by Lucien Price; this from page 135.

I think we must admit that our scale of grades does not extend far enough to include the very top men, nor the hopelessly inferior. The very best men in comparable groups are incommensurable. For all practical purposes, you will find that you will regard them as equal.

34. *Antony and Cleopatra*, act 1, scene 3.

35. Thomas Fuller's two books, *The Holy State* and *The Profane State*, are as agreeable books to take up and put down and take up again as I know. This is from *The Holy State*, book II, chapter 7. There is a fine facsimile edition with an introduction and notes by M. G. Walten published by the Columbia University Press, 1938; and again I thank Edmond Cahn for giving it to me.

36. Pascal, 69.

"The good writing that I admire," Gide wrote in his *Journal*, on June 17, 1923, "is the writing that unobtrusively arrests and detains the reader, and constrains his thought to advance but slowly. I want the reader's attention, at each step, to sink into a rich and well garnished soil. But what the reader is ordinarily after is a sort of moving carpet that carries him along with it."

38. The Thoreau is from his *Journal*, November 30, 1841.

39. The Holmes comes from *The Holmes-Laski Letters*, volume I, page 605, and volume 2, page 1061.

41. Emerson's *Journal*, October 1872. The Montaigne is in book 3, chapter 5. This is the famous chapter on "Some Verses of Virgil." You will find that I recur to it. So will you, once you read it. Take Florio's translation, which you will find in those neat little blue volumes published by Dent, unless you hold out for a more correct version, in which case, I think E. J. Trechmann's, or Jacob Zeitlin's, which Alfred A. Knopf published in 1934, the latest and the best.

42. Villon wrote:
> *"Je suis Françoys, dont ce me poise,*
> *Né de Paris emprés Pontoise,*
> *Qui, d'une corde d'une toise,*
> *Sçaura mon col que mon cul poise."*

I think the first line means, "I am François, which I find depressing." This may be wrong, but *poise* can very well mean "weigh in my mind" as well as "weigh on my neck"; and both the thought and the double use of the word is certainly characteristic of Villon.

Saintsbury's hope was expressed in the Encyclopædia Britannica, in his article on Villon.

The Pascal is 63.

247

43. My translation of the Goethe in *The Practical Cogitator* is a little different.

Roger Burlingame's book on Henry Ford was published by Alfred A. Knopf in 1954, chapter 1.

The Maitland is in volume III, page 439 of his *Collected Papers*.

44. *Henry* V, act 2, scene 3.

45. This Pascal comes from his *Treatise on Vacuum*, not from the *Pensées*.

The remark to Cynthia, from Congreve's *The Double Dealer*, act 2.

The Homer, from the *Iliad*, book 3, lines 156–160.

I took what Joan said from V. Sackville-West's *Saint Joan of Arc*.

I was listening to some architects the other day, and one of them read a passage on the Acropolis, which, he explained, came from Plutarch's life of Pericles.

"The works rose," Plutarch wrote, "tall and magnificent in size, matchless in the grace of their form. Workmen and craftsmen, artists and artisans, vied with each other, and surpassed their own technical excellence.

"Most wonderful was their speed. Each work, one would suppose, could scarcely have been completed within many succeeding generations. But they were all of them achieved within the prime of a single statesman. Agatharcus, the painter, some one reported, was boasting of the ease and speed with which he had painted his murals. Zeuxis, hearing this, remarked, 'And I of how much time I took.'

"And true it is that it is not speed and dexterity

that give weight, and stability, and niceness of beauty to a man's work, but time and labor. When time is loaned to the labor of making anything, time pays labor off in the strength and permanence of the work.

"These works raised by Pericles are the greater wonder that in so short a time they were made for such a long time. For each, in its beauty, straightway became ancient, and yet even until now each is still at its best, as fresh as when it was newly made. There is about them a perpetual newness, a perennial blooming, that seems even on close inspection to be untouched by time. It is as if the breath of an ever green and ever youthful spirit had mingled with these works."

46. *Holmes-Laski Letters*, volume 1, page 389; December 22, 1921.

The George Homans is from his book *The Human Group*, page 333.

My authorities for Tertullian's remark are H. L. Mencken's A *New Dictionary of Quotations*, page 96, and Chambers' Encyclopedia on Tertullian. Mencken cites De Carne Christi, "*Et mortuus est Dei Filius; prorsus credibile, quia ineptum est.*" Chambers gives two remarks, "*Credibile quia ineptum*" and "*Certum quia impossibile.*"

The Toynbee is in his volume 5, pages 615–618.

The logical positivists have their answer. A. J. Ayer, in an article in Encounter for October 1955, *Philosophy At Absolute Zero*, has this to say about Fate,

"Nothing indeed that actually happens can fail to be in accordance with nature. In the same admittedly trivial sense, it is impossible to cheat fate. For of anything that happens it can be said that it was fated to happen. Which shows how pointless it is to talk of fate at all. For if the only criterion that we have for deciding what is fated is what actually happens (and what other criterion could we have?), then prefixing every description of events with 'it is fated that' is an idle addition. It tells us nothing more than we already learn from the description of the event."

I can't say this explanation satisfies my curiosity, but I think Homer would have taken it as a matter of course, as trite as it was true.

47. The Acton is in a letter he wrote to Creighton on April 5, 1887.

Matthew, chapter 27, verses 55–6; Mark, chapter 15, verse 40; Luke, chapter 23, verse 49. John's account is different, chapter 19, verse 25.

48. Montaigne, book 3, chapter 5.

49. Pascal's *Pensées*, 353.

Montaigne, book 2, chapter 36, and book 3, chapter 1.

50. Thomas Fuller's *The Worthies of England*, volume 2, page 575. I hoped his account of Robin Hood would be what I had every right and reason to expect, but I was disappointed. The best, to my mind, is still Howard Pyle's, but this may be because my grandmother read it aloud to me long ago. I take it the best historical account is the chapter in Lord Raglan's *The*

Hero, where he shows that there never was such a person.

This long quotation comes from a paper that Alfred Mirsky read to a conference on "The Scientific Spirit and Democratic Faith," in New York, in May 1943. It was published by the Columbia University Press in 1944.

51. *Henry the Fourth, Part Two,* act 2, scene 2.
The Socrates is in the *Charmides,* 166E–167.

52. Montaigne, book 1, chapter 42.
This description of the onion curve is William Graham Sumner's in his *Folkways,* page 40. There's a book for you!

The scores of personality tests go on an onion curve. Read the chapters on "The Testing of Organization Man" in William H. Whyte's *The Organization Man;* Simon and Schuster, 1956; and ponder the "Appendix, How to Cheat in Personality Tests." It tells you how to get your score safely between the 40th and 60th percentiles, that is, in the bulge of the onion curve, avoiding either end. You can read more on the onion curve in volume 3 of *The World of Mathematics,* edited by James R. Newman and published by Simon and Schuster in 1956, pages 1459–1511; and on page 1481 you will find a quotation from Francis Galton which shows how close a scientist can come to believing that statistics may be a divine order.

"I know," Galton says, "of scarcely anything so apt to impress the imagination as the wonderful form of cosmic order expressed by the Law of Frequency of Error. The law would have been personified by the

Greeks and deified, if they had known of it. It reigns with serenity and in complete self-effacement, amid the wildest confusion. The huger the mob, and the greater the apparent anarchy, the more perfect is its sway. It is the supreme law of Unreason. Wherever a large sample of chaotic elements are taken in hand and marshalled in the order of their magnitude, an unsuspected and most beautiful form of regularity proves to have been latent all along."

Is there an immanent order in the universe? Almost this persuades me, to echo what Agrippa said to Paul.

53. The Wise Virgins appear in Matthew, chapter 25; the Wise Man in chapter 7.

Liddell and Scott give *integer* as the Latin for this Greek word, *akerios*, that Matthew uses. With this in mind, read Horace's ode to his friend Fuscus, the 22d in book 1, which begins, "Integer vitae . . ."; and I think you will agree that it is mistaken to translate *akerios* as "harmless."

54. Surely the best account of Alexander is Tarn's, Sir William W. Tarn, Cambridge University Press, 1948. The first of his two volumes is a Beacon paperback, 1956. The chapter on Alexander in William S. Ferguson's *Greek Imperialism*, Houghton, Mifflin, 1913, is good but hard to get.

If you think of Alexander as just a great conqueror, think again. Tarn calls him "one of the supreme fertilizing forces of history"; and adds, "He lifted the civilized world out of one groove and set it in another." Practically, consider how long it would have taken a little and nearly stamped out sect in Palestine to have gained such stature, had it not been for the common language that Alexander by his conquests and his policies spread throughout the world. He is, or ought to be, the patron saint of all Bible societies.

But what Alexander didn't do, didn't have time to do, but started, is equally or more important. Tarn concludes that "if, as many believe, there was a line of descent from his claim to divinity, through Roman Emperor and medieval Pope, to the great despotisms of yesterday, despotisms 'by the grace of God,' there is certainly a line of descent from his prayer at Apis, through the Stoics and one portion of the Christian ideal, to that brotherhood of all men which was proclaimed, though only proclaimed, in the French Revolution."

55. This piece from Sartre is out of his well-known address, *Existentialism Is a Humanism*. It was published in Paris by Les Editions Nagel in 1946. It has been translated into English at least twice: by Philip Mairet, published by Methuen and much of it reprinted in Morton White's *The Age of Analysis*, Houghton, Mifflin, 1955; and by Bernard Frechtman for the Philosophical Library. I have translated the passage I give here myself.

There seems to be a general agreement that this address is the shortest cut to a quick understanding of Existentialism, at least to the Sartre sect, for like the Protestants there are many Existentialist sects. Or you might start with Edmund Wilson's piece on Sartre in Wilson's book, *Classics and Commercials*, Farrar, Straus & Cudahy, 1950. It is also in Wilson's recent Anchor book, *A Literary Chronicle, 1920–1950*. Wilson recommends the article with which Sartre introduced the monthly magazine which he directs and which has been running since October 1945, *Les Temps Modernes* (*Modern Times*). Since, so far as I know, this has not been translated into English, I offer you a few sentences. After finding fault with literature for acting as if it could be as aloof and disinterested as pure science, Sartre says:

"It is not by running after immortality that we shall make ourselves eternal. We shall not become absolutes for having reflected in our works a few disincarnate principles, empty enough and null enough to pass from one era to another; but because we have fought passionately in our own epoch, because we have loved it passionately, and because we were willing to perish with it."

And Sartre speaks of freedom: "This freedom, you must not think of it as a metaphysical power of human "nature." [Sartre puts the word "nature" in quotes.] Nor is it a license to do whatever you want to do. Nor some sort of refuge within ourselves, within which we are free even in prison. We do not do whatever we want to do, and yet we are each of us responsible for himself. That is the fact. Man may try to explain or justify himself by causes, but the fact is, he alone supports his own weight. In this sense, freedom may very well be considered a curse; and it is a curse. But it is the sole source of human greatness."

For the philosophy of Existentialism, read the half-dozen pages in Morton White's *The Age of Analysis*; Houghton, Mifflin, 1955; and for Kierkegaard, the half-dozen pages in Henry D. Aiken's book in the same series, *The Age of Ideology*.

57. Emerson's *Journal*, June 22, 1843.

The Oppenheimer is quoted in Walter Gelhorn's book, *Security, Loyalty, and Science,* page 256; and by Alan Barth in his book, *The Loyalty of Free Men,* page 187.

You will find the Hand in Irving Dilliard's collection of *Hand, the Spirit of Liberty.* It is in the address he gave to the Elizabethan Club in New Haven on May 10, 1941.

Instead of having the gall to try to tell you what to read about freedom, I am going to ask you to sit in back behind the girls at the Sarah Lawrence College Commencement on June 7, 1956, and listen to Robert Frost. What he said was taken down, and it has since been distributed by The Fund for the Republic. Here is some of it, just as he spoke it:

"The word 'freedom' is on everybody's lips. I never have valued any liberty conferred on me particularly. I value myself on the liberties I take, and I have learned to appreciate the word 'unscrupulous.' I am not a sticker at trifles. If I wrote the history of the world in jail like Nehru twenty years ago I would expect to take many liberties with the story. I should expect to bend the story the way I wanted it to go somewhat. There is a certain measure of unscrupulousness in it. I find the same thing in good scientists. An unscrupulous person for me in science, history or literature is a person who doesn't stick at trifles.

"Now the freedom that I am asked to think about sometimes is the freedom to speak—to speak out— academic and in the press, newspapers, from the platform like this. I say I have the right to tell anything—to talk about anything I am smart enough to find out about. Second, I am free to talk about anything I am deep enough to understand, and third, I am free to talk about anything I have the ability to talk about. The limitations on my freedom, you see, are more in myself than anywhere else.

"The ability to find out, the ability to understand, the ability to express—But now that you have had more of that freedom here—and I compliment you on that—than you get in most colleges, you have reached the point of sweeping thoughts, sweeping thoughts like Toynbee's when he writes about the history of the world—you know, he leaves Vermont out—unscrupulous. But he has his point to make, and the point is the great thing, and there is the courage. There is no time when I talk or when you talk that we ought not to introduce ourselves with the expression, 'I make bold to say.' And making bold to say means leaving out what you don't want—no lies, that is corruption—but leave out what you don't want to say. . . .

"You, of course, would first prefer to think, to have the idea yourselves. I judge that from the kind of education you have had. I myself would. I am very selfish that way. I would rather think, have an idea myself, than have an idea given to me—second to my selfishness, there is an unselfishness I sometimes have, so I'll pay attention to what somebody else says to me, as you are asked to listen to me now. But the main thing is to think of it first myself."

58. The citation of the great anti-segregation opinion is Brown v. Board of Education, 347 U. S. 483. This phrase, "deliberate speed," occurs in the opinion

on the decree, 349 U. S. at page 301. I like the remark of the devout Catholic lady, who was an equally devout segregationist: "If they sit a Negro right next to me, I won't like it, but I will offer it up as a prayer. If I ever get to heaven, I'm sure God will give me the grace to put up with Negroes there." This was reported in the New York *Herald-Tribune* on February 29, 1956.

For what Senator George said, *The New York Times,* April 25, 1955.

The Hand is in the Harvard Alumni *Bulletin* for March 17, 1956.

59. Emerson's *Journal* again, this time April 11, 1834. George Weller found the title for his novel here, "Not to Eat, Not to Love."

My own favorite futility now is the doing of English crossword puzzles, for which my thanks to Sylvia Conant. I like those of Mr. Chipwinkle and Mr. Hubert Phillips, who, to my surprise, are the same person. Both books are Penguins. Let me give you a couple of examples: "It's a fairy in person"—six letters (ITSELF); "One hundred girls"—seven letters (CLASSES). Or here's one, I think from the London *Times:* "Irish author around forty"—four letters (AXLE); and another, "But a lawyer might make a fairly melting appeal to them" —three words of six, two, and seven letters (COURTS OF JUSTICE).

Anagrams play, perhaps, too large a part; e.g. "Interchange"—in five letters, is NITRE, and "Your overcoat's got shiny"—in six letters, is LUSTRE. Sometimes these English crosswords are too local for us: "It sounds like a sluggish river"—in four letters, is not the STYX, it's the OUSE. But "Arkwright was his father"—in four, has nothing to do with spinning or cotton mills; the word is SHEM. Stop me, and forgive me.

60. Daniel Sargent has pointed out to me that Paul Valéry put these two lines from Pindar as a headnote to his poem, "*Le Cimetière Marin.*" This is an elegy in a churchyard overlooking the Mediterranean, at Sète, where Valéry was born and is now buried. Pindar can very well be proud. For this poem of Valéry's has received the highest praise. Geoffrey Brereton, in his Pelican *History of French Literature* says, "The sea, the sun, the dead, the self's consciousness of them all and of its own existence, are linked in verse as sinewy and flawless as anything written in French." And Alan Chisholm, writing the article on Valéry in Chambers' Encyclopedia, says, "This is possibly the most perfect poem yet written in the twentieth century. Its wealth of imagery, its subtle meditations on death, its heroic acceptance of life despite life's flickering futility, give it an unforgettable magnificence." Which is all very well and very much to the point, except what nonsense this is about an "heroic acceptance of life!"

So much for applause. For perception and appreciation, you might start, as I did, with what Edmund Wilson says about the poem in the chapter on Valéry in *Axel's Castle*, which Scribners published in 1931, and which also contains elucidations of Yeats, Eliot, Proust, Joyce, and Rimbaud. For a translation, the one by C. Day Lewis in *Valéry's Selected Writings*, published by New Directions, 1950. Ultimately, maybe, you and I may find ourselves studying the lecture Professor Gustave Cohen gave at the Sorbonne in 1929, devoted to a detailed explanation of this one poem, "The Cemetery on the Sea." Valéry was listening inconspicuously from a far upper row of the lecture hall. It was published by Gallimard. I don't think it has been translated. If you and I ever read it, we shall then be able to make up our minds whether we like what Gustave Cohen understood as well as what we are understanding, our candle against his flare.

61. The citation for Hand's very much cited opinion in the Alcoa case is 148 Fed 2d 416; 1945. It is a long opinion. This phrase comes on page 430.

For Hector, *Troilus and Cressida,* act 4, scene 5.

The Montaigne, book 3, chapter 5, "On Some Verses of Virgil."

62. Again Emerson's *Journal;* June 1863.

I see that I have been too considerate of the altruist, as anyone who has read, or will read, Rebecca West's story, "The Salt of the Earth," will agree. It is in her volume, *The Harsh Voice;* Jonathan Cape and Doubleday, 1935.

Luke, chapter 6, verse 31; Matthew, chapter 7, verse 12.

Lord Chesterfield's letter, October 16, 1747.

George Orwell wrote this in *Polemic* for March 1947; I got it from William Empson's *The Structure of Complex Words,* New Directions, page 125.

63. The heading comes from another of Holmes's letters to Harold Laski, December 9, 1921; volume 1, page 385.

The long quotation is from Learned Hand in *The Spirit of Liberty*, Knopf, 1952; pages 62–64.

I don't know that there is anything else to be read about the Society. What do you think of it? One of the members, Judge Wyzanski, writes me: plainly, I think, on a Saturday or during recess.

"I utterly reject the fundamental philosophy of this excellent and accurate portrayal of the Society of Jobbists, its first two presidents, and its recording secretary. The trouble is that you have taken a paradox literally. Of course, when playing a game—especially if you are playing in a representative capacity—you must keep your eye on the ball, and *within the rules* try to win that game. Nothing else counts. And this is because the objects and procedure are defined. The limitations are the condition of the art. Style is performance within the prescription. Or to use a lawyer's phrase, it is 'due process.' Or to take the same thought and broaden it, we can find here the converse of Pascal's proposition: 'Tyranny is the will to have in one way what can only be had in another.' (See *The Pilgrim's Way*, anthology by my second favorite anthologist, A. T. Quiller-Couch, page 204.)

"But life is not a game. Nor is it (for me) the opposite; a struggle of deadly serious implications. That is, it is not a wager for Heaven or Hell. No such gamble is offered to man. He plays for less substantial stakes—for an ethically satisfactory life while on earth.

"Man has a chance to make a *moral* pattern—not merely something he likes, or something that has the beauty of the dance, or the virility of an ascent of Everest. If he restricts himself to what he likes and the way his taste runs, of course we may get a Learned

Hand or a Paul Valéry, but we may get Al Capone or Hitler. And to tell the young to make a pattern without at the same time telling them it is to be a moral pattern is to run the risk of which direction they arbitrarily will select. To advise them to make a *moral* choice is not to tell them *what* choice they must make. It is only to stress that in your way through life you must try to build some coherent structure drawn from the experience of the race, from your background, from your personal insight, a structure that, of course, will last hardly longer than does the theme of a sonata in the mind of the listener."

I don't agree. Morals are not wholly matters of feeling. There is a rational rectitude, even about loving your neighbor as yourself. A member of the Society of Jobbists is not confined to what he likes or to the way his taste runs. He may very well—indeed, I think he will be expected to—admit reason to its part in a moral choice. Capone or Hitler could no more be elected to the Society than Martin Luther or Savonarola. Robin Hood would be rejected on both counts.

64. The Montaigne is still more from the essay he wrote "On Some Verses from Virgil," book 3, chapter 5.

Plato's fancy is in Grote's *History of Greece*, Everyman's Edition, volume 9, page 43. I don't know where it is in Plato.

I am happy to say that I have only just now read William H. Whyte's book, *The Organization Man*, which Simon and Schuster has only just now published. Whyte explains, confirms, qualifies, and applies so much of what I have said in 62 on egoism, in 63 on jobbism, and in 64 on co-operation, and what he says gives such immediacy to so much of it, that if I had read *The Organization Man* before instead of after, I should find it hard to tell where my thoughts left off and Whyte's took over.

65. Charles Lamb wrote this to Mrs. Wordsworth on February 18, 1818.

I have quoted at length from Edward A. Shils's *The Torment of Secrecy*, The Free Press, Glencoe, Illinois, 1956, pages 21–22 and 43.

What to read on the virtues and vices of secrecy? The rest of Shils's book. And the Reports and Proceedings of the Special Subcommittee of the House of Representatives on Government Information, some of which was published in November 1956; more is to come. John E. Moss of California is the chairman.

66. More from Emerson's *Journal*, May 25, 1862.

This from Dr. Rabi is on page 469 of the official transcript. In my book, *The Oppenheimer Case*, Simon and Schuster, 1955, it is on pages 101 and 198.

Ruth Benedict's *The Chrysanthemum and the Sword*, pages 235 and 247, Houghton, Mifflin, 1954.

67. These records are as of June 1956.

Could it be that man's best endeavors succeed and surpass themselves along an onion curve? If so, what, for example, is the asymptote for the mile run? We now know that it is less than four minutes.

68. Osler's *Aequanimitas*, page 213.

70. Matthew, chapter 6, verse 11; Luke, chapter 11, verse 3.

The two versions are also distinguished rather precisely by the forms of the verb "give," as Professor W. B. Sanford has pointed out in his edition of the *Odyssey*, volume 1, page 251, Macmillan, 1950 (the best, if you want to know). Matthew uses the aorist, *dos*, a single act of giving; Luke uses *didou*, which implies "keep on giving."

Whitehead's *Adventures of Ideas*, page 19.

72. The Montaigne is near the end of chapter 8 of book 3.

73. Thornton Wilder's *Ides of March* purports to be a work of fiction. This is on page 173.

Julius Caesar, act 2, scene 2.

The Lowell is in Graham Wallas' book, *The Art of Thought*, Harcourt, Brace, 1926; pages 137–138. I don't know whether it is back in print. I buy it secondhand whenever I can.

74. Gide's *Journal*, April 2, 1929.

Henry IV, Part One, act 2, scene 3.

75. Schrödinger, *Science and Humanism*, published by the Cambridge University Press, 1951, page 49; and now in an Anchor book.

76. *Science and the Common Understanding* by J. Robert Oppenheimer, pages 75–76, Simon and Schuster, 1954. These are his Reith Lectures, which he gave in 1953 in England.

The *Journal* of the American Judicature Society for October–December 1955 has a good account of this inquiry into juries.

77. *Hamlet*, act 2, scene 2.

The Montaigne is in Florio's translation, which, as I have said, you can read in those good little volumes published by Dent; book 1, chapter 40.

The Thoreau is in his *Duty of Civil Disobedience*. We now see its gospel being performed as well as preached in Montgomery, Alabama.

78. *Paradise Lost*, book 1, verse 424.

The French quatrain is carved over the door between the supper room and the billiard room in the Tavern Club in Boston. It is quite impossible for me to translate it. Here is the brute rendering:

> *Fill up that empty glass again!*
> *Empty that full one!*
> *A thing I can't abide,*
> *Is one that's neither.*

W. W. Tarn, *Alexander the Great*, page 22; Beacon Press edition, 1956.

1 Kings, chapter 3.

80. A. Lawrence Lowell, the President of Harvard from 1909 to 1935, wrote a book, *What a University President Has Learned*. This comes from pages 16–17; Macmillan, 1938.

Sir Oliver Franks's review appeared in *The Listener* for June 14, 1956.

81. Pascal, 70.

82. *Julius Caesar*, act 2, scene 1.

William James's *Principles of Psychology*, volume I, page 274.

Sir William Watson wrote the verse.

83. Logan Pearsall Smith took this sentence of Hazlitt's from *Notes of a Journey Through France and Italy* and put it into his *Treasury of Aphorisms*, page 66. This is a good little, wise little book, the best I know; and do not neglect Smith's introduction.

To go on from 83 leads straight into the so-called paradox of Diderot: "The great poets, the great actors, and perhaps in general all the great imitators of nature, whoever they may be, endowed with imagination, with judgment, with tact, with taste—they are the most insensitive of people." Diderot wrote it up in a little dialogue, "The Paradox of the Comedian." Walter Herries Pollock's translation has recently been republished, 1957, by Hill and Wang, together with William Archer's *Masks or Faces*, and both admirably introduced and edited by Lee Strasberg.

"Actors win our hearts," Goethe said in one of his maxims, 603, "without giving up their own; their skill and their grace deceive us." So a good actor must not *live* his part. He rouses our emotions most when he does not share them. It is a straight matter of art.

Is this so? We may put this paradox to the test by applying it to an extreme case. I have never understood how it was possible for even the most gifted boy to play the part of Rosalind, or Beatrice, or Juliet, or— God rest Antony's ghost—Cleopatra. They are all the most feminine, the most female, of women. How could boys rouse an Elizabethan admiration? Here is an acute case of Diderot's paradox, where the actor not only did not, but could not "live" the part.

There must be something in this. At any rate, Goethe went much further than the Elizabethans. Goethe admired the castrati in female roles. He said, "I reflected on the reasons why these singers pleased me so greatly, and I think I have found it. In these representations, the concept of imitation and of art was invariably more strongly felt, and through their able performance a sort of conscious illusion was produced. Thus a double pleasure is given, in that these persons are not women, but only represent women. The young men have studied the properties of the female sex in its being and behaviour; they know them thoroughly and reproduce them like an artist; they represent, not themselves, but a nature absolutely foreign to them." This is quoted in a recent book, *The Castrati in Opera*, by Angus Heriot, published by Secker and Warburg, page 26.

To go on a little further, I suggest, oddly enough, a chapter in a book on the doctrine of the Trinity. It is by Dorothy L. Sayers, whose detective stories you probably have read and, if you are interested in Dante, whose *Introductory Papers on Dante* you ought to read —Methuen, 1954. She is now translating the *Comedy* for the Penguins. Her book on the Trinity is called *The Mind of the Maker*—Harcourt, Brace, 1941, and a Meridian book—and the chapter I refer to is called "Scalene Trinities." In it Miss Sayers applies the doctrine of the Trinity to the human artist, for God made man in His own image. But the human triangle of the Trinity is not equilateral. It's askew in the best artist,

266

and so scalene. There is the father-ridden, who thinks he can do without the technique on which the son-ridden wholly relies, and there is the ghost-ridden writer who "conceives that the emotion which he feels is in itself sufficient to awaken response, without undergoing discipline of a thorough incarnation . . ." You see, it is the son-ridden that Diderot and Goethe so much too much admire and the ghost-ridden they look at askance. You won't be any more bothered by the theology than I was; and for theologians there is an alluring page applying the ancient heresies, Arianism, Manichaeism, etc., to art.

84. Lawrence J. Henderson's book on Pareto was published in 1935 by the Harvard University Press. This sentence is on pages 46–47; read also pages 110–115. George C. Homans wrote the best book on Pareto (in which I collaborated), page 271 ff.; and for Pareto himself, section 2068. Henderson recommends Walter B. Cannon's *The Wisdom of the Body*, and I heartily concur.

Hampshire's book on Spinoza is a Penguin. My quotation is on page 122.

85. All this is from W. V. Quine's book *From a Logical Point of View*, pages 42–46, published by the Harvard University Press in 1953.

86. *Troilus and Cressida*, act 3, scene 2.

Russell's *Human Knowledge*, page 478, published by Simon and Schuster in 1948.

The Eliot is in his little book on Dante.

87. The Whitehead is in *The Concept of Nature,* page 163; Cambridge University Press, 1920 and 1955. Ferris Greenslet and I used the last sentence in *The Practical Cogitator,* but we did not know where it came from until Dr. Philip Shen told us.

The Quine, *From a Logical Point of View,* page 79.

Thoreau's *Journal,* September 29, 1842, volume I, page 449.

The Poincaré is quoted by Hadamard in his book on *The Psychology of Invention,* on page 31. Hadamard's own remarks are on page 127. The Princeton University Press published this book in 1945; the Dover Publications, in 1954. Though it does not purport to be a How-to-do-it, that is what it is.

88. This is from the *Hermotimus* of Lucian, one of his best dialogues. E. R. Bevan, in his *Stoics and Sceptics,* Clarendon Press, 1913, on page 138, calls it "a little work not unworthy to be set with Plato's." Walter Pater made a chapter out of most of it for his *Marius the Epicurean,* but he did not include this passage. Nor did he credit Lucian. The *Hermotimus* is not in the Lucian in the Loeb Library. So I have consulted the translation of H. W. and F. G. Fowler, volume 2, page 84; Clarendon Press, 1905, which John J. Chapman uses in his admirable—how could it not be?— little book, *Lucian, Plato, and Greek Morals*; Houghton, Mifflin, 1931.

You know Fowler. H. W. Fowler wrote that best of all books on how to read and write, *Modern English Usage*; he and his brother made the Concise Oxford Dictionary.

Do you know Sir Ernest Gowers' books, *Plain*

Words and *The ABC of Plain Words?* The best since Fowler.

Tobias Dantzig's book, *Number, the Language of Science*, Macmillan, 1930; and now an Anchor book. My quotation is from the Anchor edition, page 249.

89. I don't know the reference in Galileo. I took this from Herbert Dingle's Eddington Lecture, Cambridge University Press, 1954, page 59. You'll have to ask Giorgio de Santillana, M.I.T., Cambridge, Massachusetts.

Schrödinger's *What Is Life and Other Scientific Essays*, page 226; another Anchor book. The *Odyssey*, VIII, 43.

90. Matthew Arnold, *On Translating Homer*.

The first quotation is from Benjamin Lee Whorf's article in the April 1941 number of the *Technology Review*. The Foreign Service Institute of the Department of State reprinted it in 1950, which is how I got it. Give the Department credit for publishing one of the important works on meaning. Whorf's *Selected Writings* have recently been published; I've not yet seen it.

The Quine is more *From a Logical Point of View*, this from pages 78–79.

91. Thoreau's *Journal*, March 22, 1842; and *All's Well That Ends Well*, act 4, scene 3.

Max Radin, in his *Law As Logic and Experience*, page 18.

92. Luke, chapter 15, verse 7.

The Toynbee remark, volume 5, page 439.

The William James, his *Varieties of Religious Experience;* Longmans, Green, 1902, pages 127–128. Is there any better book on religion? I doubt it. Frazer's *Golden Bough?* Salomon Reinach's *Orpheus?*

For the early history of Christianity, there may be something better than Kirsopp Lake's *Landmarks of Early Christianity,* Macmillan, 1922; but if there is, I don't know it, and I doubt it. Anyhow, set beside the Four Gospels Plato's *Crito, Phaedo,* and *The Republic;* and I suggest the translation of W. H. D. Rouse, a Mentor book; or Cornford's somewhat abridged translation of *The Republic.*

The Whitehead, in the *Dialogues,* by Lucien Price, page 92.

93. Lord Goddard's remark in the House of Lords was reported in *The New York Times* on July 11, 1956.

94. *The Listener* of June 14, 1956, gives the whole talk.

The long quotation is from Bertrand Russell's *A History of Western Philosophy,* page 827; Simon and Schuster.

Matthew, chapter 23, verse 12; Luke, chapter 14, verse 11 and chapter 18, verse 14.

95. Pascal, 4.

96. *Hamlet,* act 5, scene 1.

The quotations from the Gospels are from Luke, chapter 17, verse 33; Luke, chapter 9, verse 24; Matthew, chapter 16, verse 25; Mark, chapter 8, verse 35.

And, at the end, *Much Ado About Nothing,* act 4, near the end of scene 2.

97. Pascal, 4 and 331.
On page 15 of *The Tragic Sense of Life;* Macmillan, 1926.

98. This is from Dorothy M. Emmet's *The Nature of Metaphysical Thinking,* page 132; Macmillan, 1949. I was given this book in Arizona by Blair, of Blair's Book Shop in Tucson, and I cherish it because I think it took me as near to an understanding of metaphysics as I ever hope to get.

The two Holmes, from *Ideals and Doubts,* 1915, and *Natural Law,* 1918. Both are in the *Collected Legal Papers.*

The quotation from Reinhold Niebuhr I found in Will Herberg's book, *Protestant-Catholic-Jew, an Essay in American Religious Sociology;* Doubleday, 1955, page 282.

Didn't William Empson write a poem about two mirrors facing each other?

99. Pierre Champion's edition of the trial, volume 2, page 42, Paris, 1921; Paul Doncoeur's *La Minute Française des Interrogatoires de Jeanne La Pucelle,* Melun, 1952, pages 97–105; and Régine Pernoud's *Vie et Mort de Jeanne d'Arc,* Hachette, 1953, page 211. There is an English translation of the Pernoud by J. M. Cohen, published by Methuen–Harcourt, Brace, 1955.

If Joan's admirable reply was a quotation, so too was the Cry on the Cross—see 40; and neither was the less for being so. And so too perhaps what Latimer said to Ridley—1.

100. I got all this about Joan from Régine Pernoud's book on the Rehabilitation Trial, *Vie et Mort de Jeanne d'Arc*, pages 60, 229 and 253.

What to read on Joan? Surely the play by George Bernard Shaw. The life by V. Sackville-West, distributed by the Literary Guild in 1936. Mark Twain wrote a book on her. So did Anatole France. So did Andrew Lang. All we really know came out in her two trials, one when she was condemned and burned, and at which she testified herself; the other twenty years later at which she was rehabilitated, her friends testifying for her and her enemies, as many as were left, testifying for themselves. Joan was canonized in 1920, four years before Shaw put her on the stage.

101. I take this from Frederick Chamberlin's *The Sayings of Queen Elizabeth*, John Lane, 1923, page 142.

102. This is from a lecture Walt Whitman gave in 1879, on April 14. Harrison Tweed sent it to me in Maxwell Geismar's *The Whitman Reader*, a Cardinal book. God bless Whitman for being on the top of that omnibus! I don't think anyone else could have given us this.

103. Selden, in his *Table Talk*; Shakespear in his *Second Part of Henry VI*, act 4, scene 2.

Justice Felix Frankfurter sent me Sir William Harcourt's letter. I tried to cut it and failed. It is in Gardiner's *Life of Sir William Harcourt*, London, 1923, pages 607–608.

104. About Beatrice, see the *Paradiso:* VII, 17; XV, 34; and XXX, 26.

For Hephaistos passing the wine, the *Iliad*, I, 599; for Ares and Aphrodite, the *Odyssey*, VIII, 326.

The Whitehead is in Lucien Price's *Dialogues*, page 199.

105. The Bohr comes from his address at the Bicentennial of Columbia University, in October 1954; Doubleday published it with other addresses in 1955, under the title, *The Unity of Knowledge*, edited by Lewis Leary, page 60.

106. The Montaigne is about two thirds of the way through chapter 5 in book 3.

The Plato is in *The Laws*, book 7.

The quotation is from Claudian's *Entropius*, book 1, verse 24.

107. The two occasions on which Odysseus wept are *Odyssey*, book 8, verses 83 ff., and book 5, verses 150 ff. I have no doubt there were others.

108. This Whitehead is on page 213 ff. of his *Adventures of Ideas*.

"As flies to wanton boys . . . ," *Lear*, act 4, scene 1.

The Jesus is in John, chapter 9, the first three verses.

The remark to Theodorus is in Plato's *Theaetetus*, 176A.

The Skinner is from an article in *The American Scholar*, the 1955–1956 winter issue.

109. *Hamlet*, act 2, scene 2. See 77.

The Montaigne is more from book 3, chapter 5.

The first Holmes is from the speech he gave at Harvard on Memorial Day, 1895, called "A Soldier's Faith." The second Holmes is from the end of an article called "Natural Law," in the *Collected Legal Papers*. The letter to Laski is dated February 6, 1925, volume I, page 706.

INDEX

A

absolution, 197

abstraction, expressing an attitude, 56

acceptance of possibility of the worst, 141

achievement and creation, 145

Acropolis, building, 248–249

Across the River and Into the Trees (Hemingway), 33

activities, useless, 113–115

Acton, Lord, on power corruption, 88

actor, living his part, 265–266

Adams, John, 120

admiration, dramatic, 66

Adventures of Ideas (Whitehead), 223, 238–239, 273; *quoted,* 141–142

adversary process, 111

advice, giving and receiving, 101–103

Aesculapius, 116

Agatharcus, 248

Age of Ideology, The (Aiken), 254

Aiken, Henry D., 254

Alcoa monopoly case, 118, 259

Alexander the Great:
cutting the Gordian knot, 162
greatness, 91, 252
line of descent, 253
Parmenion's advice, 103

all or none, 161–162

All Quiet on the Western Front (Remarque) 132

All's Well That Ends Well (Shakespear), *quoted,* 189

Alsop, Joseph and Stewart, 165

alternatives, 167–168

altruism:
complete, 120–121
moral risk of, 20
Nature takes care of, 123
Society of Jobbists, 124

Americans, faith in faith, 202

B

Browning, Robert, on poet's right of privacy, 241
Brunschvicg, L. C., 199
buildings, grace of, 31
Bundy, McGeorge, 237
Burbage, James, 78
Burlingame, Roger, 74, 248

C

Caesar, Julius, mind, 146
Caesar, Julius (Shakespear), *quoted*, 168
Cahn, Edmond, on Jehovah's laughter, 219–220
cake, eating and having, 161
Cannon, Walter B., 267
Carcassonne, France, 81
Carpentier, Georges, 31
Carson, Ralph M., 244
castrati, in female roles, 266
Castrati in Opera, The (Heriot), *quoted*, 266
casuistry, 196
cat, verses about, *quoted*, 160

Catholic Church, Specific Authority rule, 244–245
Cato, 164
cause, devotion to, 230
Cecil, Henry, 22, 238
"Cemetery on the Sea, The" (Valéry), 258
Chamberlin, Frederick, 272
Chapman, John J., 268
on Shakespear's Sonnets, 242
Characteristics (Hazlitt), 240
charity, 121
"Charmides" (Socrates), 96
Chaucer, Geoffrey, 42, 241
Chesterfield, Lord, the Golden Rule, 122
Chicago University Law School, wire-tapping jury deliberations, 155
Chisholm, Alan, on Valéry's poem, 258
Choate, Rufus, on the Declaration of Independence, 55
chorus, being a part of, 129
Christian doctrine, 105
Christianity:
essence of, 225
power of, 226

278

D

E

wanting and having, 129

French Literature, History of (Brereton), *quoted*, 258

Frenchmen, facts and beliefs, 17

Freud, Sigmund:
on the meaning of *Lear*, 122
pleasure-ego, 102

Friends at Court (Cecil), 238; *quoted*, 22

From a Logical Point of View (Quine), 243; *quoted*, 174–176, 180–181, 188

Frost, Robert, on freedom, 255–256

Fuller, Thomas, 246, 250

futilities, favorite, 257

future and past, 79–83

G

Galileo, telescope, 138

Galton, Francis, on form of cosmic order, 251–252

Garrison, William Lloyd, 120

Geismar, Maxwell, 272

Gelhorn, Walter, 255

generalities, 56

gentling rats, 94–95

George, Senator Walter F., on disagreement, 112

Gide, André, on good writing, 246

Glance Toward Shakespeare, A (Chapman), *quoted*, 242

Goddard, Lord, on avenging crime, 192, 270

Gods, laughter of, 217

Goethe, Johann Wolfgang von:
on actors' art, 265, 267
autobiography, 82
on castrati in female roles, 266
Faust, 217–218
on getting what one asks for, 127
on memory, 73–74, 75
on occasional verses, 39
private life, 46
on thinking, 136
on understanding, 6

Golden Bough, The (Frazer), 270

Golden Key to Open Hidden Treasure, A (Brooks), 28

Golden Mean, 89

Golden Rule, 121, 122

good and evil, antithetical, 224–225

Gorki, Maxim, 233

285

I

J

K

M

N

O

Q

R

Rabelais, François, meeting with Villon, 71

Rabi, Isidor Isaac, on Oppenheimer, 135–136, 262

Radin, Max, on freedom of action, 190

Raglan, Lord, 250

rats, care of, 92–94

Ravenshoe (Kingsley), *quoted*, 72

reading:
  sharing with author, 3
  speed, 63

Reflections of a Physicist (Bridgman), 239; *quoted*, 26–27

Reinach, Salomon, 270

Reist, Adolph, 139

religion, interim ethics, 141–142

Religious Experience, Varieties of (James), 270; *quoted*, 191

Renan, Joseph Ernest, on scientific taste, 182

renunciation, 122

repentance, 190–192

Republic, The (Plato), 20, 270

republics, internal diversity, 171

rhetoric, mother of lies, 61

RIAS (West Berlin Radio), 58

Richard II (Shakespear), *quoted*, 141

Richards, Ivor Armstrong, 234, 235, 239, 243
  on suspension of disbelief, 13
  on toil of grace, 30

Ridley, Nicholas, 232

Rilke, Rainer Maria, 233, 240

Rimbaud, Arthur, 258

ripeness is all, 37, 240

Robin Hood, 92, 250

Robinson, James Harvey, on monkeying around, 109–110

Robinson, Sugar Ray, 31

Romeo and Juliet (Shakespear), *quoted*, 41

Roosevelt, Franklin Delano, 16, 58, 237

Rotary International, motto, 121–122

Rouse, W. H. D., 270

Russell, Bertrand, 270
  on natural laws, 177

S

Sackville-West, Victoria, 248

T

U

Unamuno y Jugo, Miguel de, on philosophers, 200–201
unanimity, generalities, 165
understanding:
  advances in, 5
  learning, 6–8
  meaning of, 1
  outruns expression, 3
  process, 2, 177–179
understatements, 62
United States Supreme Court, desegregation, 111
Unity of Knowledge, The (Leary), 273
University Professor Has Learned, What a (Lowell), 264; *quoted*, 164–165
unscrupulousness, 255
useless activities, 113–115

V

Vacuum, Treatise on (Pascal), 248; *quoted*, 79

Valéry, Paul:
  "*Cimetière Marin, Le,*" 258–259
  on truth, 237
Valéry's Selected Writings, 258
Varieties of Religious Experience (James), 270; *quoted*, 191
Vermeer, Jan, 82
vicarian, moral risks of, 20–21
Viereck, Peter, 118
Villon, François, *quoted*, 71, 247
Viollet Le Duc, Eugène Emmanuel, 81
virtue, excess of a, 91
Voltaire (François Marie Arouet), 233
"Virgil, Some Verses of" (Montaigne), 247; *quoted*, 69, 90, 119, 130

W

Wallas, Graham, 147
Walpole, Hugh, 230
Walten, M. G., 246
Warren, Earl, desegregation cases, 111
Washington, George, 149

302

ABOUT THE AUTHOR

*Aphorisms and apothegms have had to compete
with the practice of the law, with scholarship, with
big-game hunting in Africa, and with writing for
time and interest in Charles P. Curtis' life. Educated at Groton, Harvard, and the Ecole des
Sciences Politiques in Paris, he has taught government and sociology at Harvard, served as a member
of the Harvard Corporation, and been a member of
that university's Society of Fellows. His published
legal studies include* Lions Under the Throne *and*
It's Your Law. *With George C. Homans he wrote*
Introduction to Pareto *and with his brother, Richard C. Curtis,* Hunting in Africa, East and West.
He is also author of The Oppenheimer Case: The
Trial of a Security System, *published in 1955, and
with Ferris Greenslet he edited in 1945 the much-
loved anthology for thinkers called* The Practical
Cogitator.